The Spiritual Warrior's Guide to

DEFEATING
WATER SPIRITS

Other Books by Jennifer LeClaire

The Spiritual Warfare Battle Plan

Angels on Assignment Again

Evenings With the Holy Spirit

Releasing the Angels of Abundant Harvest

Waging Prophetic Warfare

Revival Hubs Rising

Jezebel's Puppets: Exposing the Agenda of False Prophets

The Next Great Move of God

Mornings With the Holy Spirit

Satan's Deadly Trio

The Making of a Prophet

The Spiritual Warrior's Guide to Defeating Jezebel

Developing Faith for the Working of Miracles

Did the Spirit of God Say That?

Breakthrough!

Fervent Faith

A Prophet's Heart

Faith Magnified

The Heart of the Prophetic

JENNIFER LECLAIRE

The Spiritual Warrior's Guide to

DEFEATING
WATER SPIRITS

Overcoming Demons

That Twist, Suffocate, and Attack

God's Purposes for Your Life

DESTINY IMAGE® PUBLISHERS, INC.
P.O. Box 310, Shippensburg, PA 17257-0310
"Promoting Inspired Lives."

This book and all other Destiny Image and Destiny Image Fiction books are available at Christian bookstores and distributors worldwide.

Cover design by: Eileen Rockwell

For more information on foreign distributors, call 717-532-3040.

Or reach us on the Internet: www.destinyimage.com

ISBN 13 TP: 978-0-7684-4294-6

ISBN 13 EBook: 978-0-7684-4295-3

Large Print ISBN: 978-0-7684-4296-0

Hard Cover ISBN: 978-0-7684-4297-7

For Worldwide Distribution, Printed in the U.S.A.

2 3 4 5 6 / 21 20 19 18

Dedication

This book is dedicated to the often-rejected spiritual warfare voices who warned us about marine demons long before most of the Body of Christ was willing to accept their reality. I pray this book helps to vindicate you from the persecution you faced in exposing these water spirits and adds to the small body of resources available on these submarine foes.

Acknowledgments

I'm so grateful for Larry Sparks' foresight and vision to publish a book like *The Spiritual Warrior's Guide to Defeating Water Spirits*. Let's face it; marine demons are not exactly mainstream spiritual warfare—but they are just as real and just as active as the principalities and powers we've heard much more about. Thanks to Larry, Don Nori Jr., and the Destiny Image team for understanding how vital it is to get the word out about these nefarious demons in this hour. I decree and declare you are prophetic forerunners for a new generation of spiritual warfare revelation.

Contents

Foreword

Every believer will face spiritual warfare in their life at some time. It is important to arm yourself with knowledge to prevail against the works of hell. Many saints either do not properly discern demonic attack or employ the wrong strategy. These two mistakes can lead to swift defeat. This book will help you gain strategy and wisdom to defeat the enemy. Jennifer LeClaire has packaged revelation to further your understanding of spiritual warfare.

It is imperative that God's people are well armed to rise and conquer the attacks of the enemy. This is one of the reasons I and many others have dedicated a major part of our lives to equipping God's people in these areas. Apostle Paul warned us not to fight an infective battle: *"Therefore I run in such a way, as not without aim; I box in such a way, as not beating the air"* (1 Corinthians 9:26).

Paul did not beat the air! He knew by revelation how to defeat the powers of darkness. Many believers are unaware of the tactics of the enemy. They are in constant attack mode with no real strategy or effective wisdom. They are depleted and discouraged because of unnecessary and ineffective warfare. This book will release understanding to overcome the entanglements of the enemy.

I have enjoyed Jennifer LeClaire's writing for a number of years. She has been a strong advocate in the area of spiritual warfare and prophetic revelation. She has a real passion to release timely messages with established biblical truths. She also knows how to pull back the curtain and take a fresh prophetic look at various subjects.

In this latest book on marine demons, Jennifer once again provides a prophetic glimpse into the realm of darkness with tools to defeat these demons! She identifies evil spirits and gives her readers insightful teaching to overcome attacks. This wisdom is for every spiritual warrior. Get ready for an eye-opening journey as you turn these pages. Jennifer has penned another must-read book!

It is time that you conquer and overcome the lies of the enemy! You have been called to experience victory. God has great plans for you. The enemy will try to stop you, but you can break his grip and put his minions under your feet. No marine demon should be able to stop the plans of God's advancing army. No water spirit should effectively bind up a city or region when God's ruling people exercise their authority. It is time to get off the sideline, get activated, and take your place. It is time to fight for your city, family, and nation. It is time to stand boldly on the Word of God with authority and faith. It is time to remind the devil of the victory at Calvary. Marine demons must bow!

There are not many books written on this subject; it is a subject that is unknown to many believers. You will be surprised by the truths revealed in this book. I pray that as you read the Lord will give you understanding in all things. You will have insight that you did not have before. Be blessed as you receive revelation from the pen of Jennifer LeClaire.

John Eckhardt
Bestselling author, *Prayers That Rout Demons*

Introduction

When you picked up this book you may have wondered, *What in the world is Jennifer talking about? I thought Jezebel was the queen bee of the demon world.*

I used to think the same thing. In fact, I was taught that Jezebel, witchcraft, and religion were our three main spiritual foes. Besides fear, demons, and voices of rejection, those three spiritual warfare rock stars, in my mind, were responsible for wreaking most of the havoc in the earth today. Although I thought at that time I was well-equipped, I was ignorant of many of the devil's devices.

Of course, I am still learning—we all are. I find it haughty and foolish to proclaim anyone as an "expert" in any specific demon spirit. There are leading voices in the spiritual warfare teaching movement, as well as emerging voices. There are generals in the battlefield. But we are all learning and growing and my experience with water spirits even while writing this book reminded me of that reality.

When I was hyperfocused on Jezebel, witchcraft, and religion, I had never heard of such a thing as a Python spirit, much less a Behemoth. I never considered there were, as the late spiritual warfare teacher Derek Prince called them, "persons without bodies" dwelling beneath the surface of seas, ravines, lakes, rivers, streams, and other waters around the world.

As I matured in the Lord and spent time around seasoned, battle-tested warriors who taught me the importance of spiritual discernment, I learned that there are many unseen forces in the spirit world—some that roam the earth like a roaring lion and some that call the waters their domain.

My first encounter with a water spirit was Python, which you can read about in Acts 16. Paul went toe-to-toe with this demon and took a beating before he was ultimately set free to the glory of God. Paul gained the victory, but not without some pain. I imagine it was the first time the apostle encountered this variety of marine demon.

I can relate to Paul's battle with Python because the same thing happened to me. I didn't end up beaten and put in jail, but I ended up beaten down and in bondage until I learned how to fight this serpentine beast. When you encounter an unfamiliar enemy, you are, well, unfamiliar with what is manifesting against you. You may call out a spirit you've battled before in ignorance, unknowingly bringing more spiritual warfare on your head.

When I received the revelation that marine demons were real, I decided to take Paul's advice and "not be ignorant of the devil's devices" (see 2 Corinthians 2:11). I decided to study to show myself approved (see 2 Timothy 2:15) or you might say study to survive the fierce battle raging against me. After spending most of my Christian life fighting Jezebel, witchcraft, and religion, I understood this enemy class—water spirits—had an advantage on me because I didn't know they existed or how to fight them.

Since then, I've faced Rahab spirits—mostly in my international travels—I've faced Leviathan spirits, squid spirits, and more. I've taken a few hits and gained a lot of wisdom. My eyes have been opened to the severity of the strongholds marine demons have in certain areas of the world—and on certain people's minds and bodies.

I've written this book in hopes of taking the mask off marine demons—nefarious creatures in the waters of the earth that attack unsuspecting (and at times undiscerning) believers. I pray this book opens your eyes to the invisible enemies that may be attacking you and influencing souls in your city.

Chapter 1

WAGING
WARFARE UNDER WATER

S CIENTISTS say most adults don't remember much before the age of
seven. Although experiences in infancy and childhood shape our personalities in ways we don't discern, a form of amnesia sets in by first or
second grade. Youthful memories grow strangely dim—unless it was a trau-
matic event. That explains why I have few memories of my early childhood
but vividly recall a near-death experience in the water.

When I was about three years of age, my parents took us on a family vaca-
tion to Daytona Beach, a city known for NASCAR and hard, sand-packed
beaches on the "Fun Coast" of Florida. I didn't comprehend it then—and in
fact only recently came to understand the powers of evil at work—but a water
spirit tried to drown me. I'll always remember the feeling of terror as unseen
forces pulled me under the water. I'll never forget the overwhelming feeling
of confusion and helplessness that gripped my young soul.

Thank God, my parents rescued me from the water spirit's deadly agenda.
It wasn't negligence on their part. I had floaties around my arms and they
were watching over me carefully. An invisible enemy lured me to jump in the

water and pulled me under violently. Water mythology—the study of legendary water creatures—offers insight into the attack.

We have to understand at the outset that not all mythological stories are tied to spirit realm realities—but many are. Mythmakers didn't have the spiritual discernment or Holy Spirit knowledge to understand what they were seeing manifest with their natural eyes—the strange deaths or failed crops or colossal storms at sea—so they attributed what was often the work of demons to gods and goddesses, and other creatures they could not readily observe.

Scandinavian mythology, for example, speaks of a water spirit named Fossegrim that lured women and children into lakes and streams to drown them. And Slavic mythology points to Vodianoi, which appeared as old men with long green beards covered in scales that caused swimmers to drown. Is it really possible a water spirit targeted me? I believe so. Many times, the enemy sees markings of a call on your life and attacks you at a young age, while you are innocent and unable to fight back.

Again, while some myths are just myths, I am convinced many mythological beings are actual demon powers that have operated in the earth since one-third of the angels joined lucifer in his insurrection. When lucifer rose up in pride against Jehovah, he and his cohorts suddenly found themselves cast out of Heaven into the second heaven.

Peter describes an enemy that roams about like roaring lions seeking someone to devour (see 1 Peter 5:8), but some of these demons are swimming in the water realm seeking to kill, steal, and destroy the lives of those who are ignorant to their operations. One of the ways water spirits kill, steal, and destroy is through drowning.

According to the Florida Department of Health, Florida has the highest drowning rate in the nation for children under four years of age. Parents are wise to teach pool safety and enroll their tots in swimming lessons—but when water spirits strike, these practical lessons do little good to combat dark forces. Of course, drowning is an extreme manifestation of a water spirit attack. Water spirits attack in many ways, as we'll see through the chapters of this book. I believe the pages ahead will open your eyes to some of the assaults against your mind, body, and relationships.

Indeed, for all the talk of principalities and powers like Jezebel and witchcraft, many spiritual warriors are less familiar with water spirits lurking in oceans, rivers, ravines, lakes, brooks, streams, and other bodies of water. From Python to Leviathan to Dagon to Rahab and beyond, many spiritual warriors like you are feeling the effects of water spirits and don't know what is harassing or hindering them. Because the church has not taught much on marine demons, many are essentially ignorant of these demonic devices (see 2 Corinthians 2:11).

Before we move into the deep truths about water spirits, it's vital that we understand the biblical principles of spiritual warfare and the significance of water in the Bible.

Our Struggle Isn't Just in the Heavens

Paul the apostle lays out the hierarchy of demons in Ephesians 6:12: *"For our struggle is not against flesh and blood, but against the rulers, against the powers, against the world forces of this darkness, against the spiritual forces of wickedness in the heavenly places."*

As I wrote in my book, *Jezebel's Puppets,* spiritual warfare requires wrestling—hand-to-hand combat with bodiless enemies we can't see with our natural eyes. The Greek word for "wrestling" in Ephesians 6:12 is *pallo.* The *New Testament Greek Lexicon* defines it as "a contest between two in which each endeavors to throw the other, and which is decided when the victor is able to hold his opponent down with his hand upon his neck; the term is transferred to the Christian's struggle with the power of evil."

Demons try to choke you—or put you in a stranglehold. In the wrestling world, a stranglehold is an illegal hold that chokes the opponent.

Merriam-Webster calls it a "force or influence that chokes or suppresses freedom of movement or expression." If the wrestler doesn't break free from the stranglehold, the lack of blood or air can cause him to black out. Translating this to our spiritual realities, the enemy wants to choke the Word of God out of your mouth so you can't wield your sword of the Spirit or pray. The enemy wants to choke out the revelation of who you are in Christ and your authority over him.

In Ephesians 6:12, you can see there are differing, broad categories of demon powers. Let's start with principalities. The word "principality" comes from the Greek word *arche*. In Ephesians 6:12, principalities refer to "the first place, principality, rule, magistracy" and speaks of "angels and demons," according to *The King James Version (KJV) New Testament Greek Lexicon*. *Vine's Expository Dictionary* gives more insight, calling principalities "supramundane beings who exercise rule."

Exouisa is the Greek word for "powers" in Ephesians 6:12. Our lexicon defines it as "the leading and more powerful among created beings superior to main, spiritual potentates." Meanwhile, "ruler," which comes from the Greek word *kosmokrator,* means "lord of the world, prince of this age," and wickedness from the Greek.

Ponēria, which means unrighteousness, wickedness, greed, fornication, covetousness, and malice, is the Greek word for "wickedness" in this verse is. *Merriam-Webster's* definition of malice is "a desire to cause pain, injury, or distress to another," or "intent to commit an unlawful act or cause harm without legal justification or excuse."

The Greek word *kosmokrator* is used to describe "rulers of the darkness of this world," which means "lord of the world, prince of this age." And darkness stems from Greek word *skotos,* which can mean darkness, like night darkness. However, in the context of Ephesians 6:12, it means "of ignorance respecting divine things and human duties, and the accompanying ungodliness and immorality, together with their consequent misery in hell." It also means, "persons in whom darkness becomes visible and holds sway," according to *The KJV New Testament Greek Lexicon.*

Our struggle is not just with demons in heavenly places. It's also with demons in watery places. The good news is, you have authority over every demon power—on the earth, over the earth, and in the seas.

The Wonders of Water in the Word

The Word of God speaks of the water of life, rivers of living water, passing through the waters, springs of waters unto eternal life. We find literal stories about water and important metaphors that are worth exploring as we seek to understand water spirits. The law of first mention—a principle that suggests the first place in Scripture a word or doctrine is found informs our understanding of God's intent—is a strategic place to start our study.

The first time we see water mentioned in the Bible is in the second verse of Genesis. Genesis 1:2 tells us, *"The earth was formless and void, and darkness was over the surface of the deep, and the Spirit of God was moving over the surface of the waters."*

This is an especially telling verse in the context of the law of first mention. We see a spirit—the Spirit of God—moving over the surface of the waters. Given the enemy always works to counterfeit what God has done or is doing, we understand that demon spirits will move over the waters to combat God's purposes and plans in the earth. This is the best case for marine demons—but it's not the only one.

Searching the Bible, we find Scriptures that connect water with both death and life. Isaiah 12:3 speaks of drawing water from the wells of salvation with joy. Jesus promised everyone who believes in Him would see rivers of living water flowing from His heart (John 7:38). In Isaiah 43:2, God makes a beautiful promise: *"When you pass through the waters, I will be with you; and through the rivers, they will not overflow you...."*

God refers to Himself as *"the fountain of living waters"* in Jeremiah 2:13. We are baptized with water as a sign of being buried and resurrected to new life in Jesus (see 1 Peter 3:21). David spoke of God leading him beside quiet, or still, waters (see Psalm 23:2) and Paul talks of washing of the water with the Word (see Ephesians 5:26). We know Naaman dipped seven times in the Jordan River by the word of the prophet Elisha and was healed of his leprosy (see 2 Kings 5). In heaven, there's a river of the water of life (see Revelation 22:1-2). These are just a few of the many Scriptures that speak of the life-giving, cleansing or healing power of water.

Also enlightening as we set out to expose and defeat water spirits is the reality that water is a symbol of the Holy Spirit in Scripture. Jesus was speaking of the Spirit of God when He told the woman at the well, *"Everyone who drinks of this water will thirst again; but whoever drinks of the water that I will give him shall never thirst; but the water that I will give him will become in him a well of water springing up to eternal life"* (John 4:13-14).

Water archetypes paint vivid pictures through Scripture, including physical birth (see Genesis 1:20), purification (see Ezekiel 36:25; Hebrews 10:22), God's help (see Isaiah 8:6); personal posterity (see Isaiah 48:1) and humankind's purposes (see Proverbs 20:5).

Water is overwhelmingly positive in Scripture, but water can also carry a negative connotation—including enemy attack. Second Samuel 22:17-18 tells us, *"He sent from on high, He took me; He drew me out of many waters. He delivered me from my strong enemy, from those who hated me, for they were too strong for me."* Psalm 144:7-8 shares, *"Stretch forth Your hand from on high; rescue me and deliver me out of great waters, out of the hand of aliens whose mouths speak deceit, and whose right hand is a right hand of falsehood."*

And Psalm 124 reads:

> *"Had it not been the Lord who was on our side,"* let Israel now
> say, *"Had it not been the Lord who was on our side when men*

rose up against us, then they would have swallowed us alive, when their anger was kindled against us; then the waters would have engulfed us the stream would have swept over our soul; then the raging waters would have swept over our soul." Blessed be the Lord, who has not given us to be torn by their teeth. Our soul has escaped as a bird out of the snare of the trapper; the snare is broken and we have escaped. Our help is in the name of the Lord, who made heaven and earth."

Overwhelming Water Facts

It's interesting to note that most of the earth is actually water, and much of the earth's population is surrounded by water, including seas, rivers, streams, and lakes.

About 71 percent of the earth's surface is covered in water, according to the United States Geological Survey,[1] and oceans, seas, and bays make up nearly 97 percent of the earth's water. The remaining 3 percent are lakes, swamp water, rivers, ice caps, ground water, and atmospheric water. Noteworthy is the scientific fact that water is not only *on* the earth but *in* the earth.

Likewise, our bodies are made up of about 60 percent water, the USGS reports. H.H. Mitchell, in the *Journal of Biological Chemistry 158*,[2] breaks this down further: the brain and heart are composed of 73 percent water, and the lungs are about 83 percent water. The skin contains 64 percent water, muscles and kidneys are 79 percent, and our bones are 31 percent water.

Like blood, water is essential to life. Water offers nutrients to cells, regulates internal body temperature, metabolizes food, flushes waste, serves as a shock absorber, forms saliva, and lubricates our joints. It's no wonder the enemy seeks a stronghold in the water realm.

How Marine Demons Pollute
God's Purposes for Water

Satan is not a creator. He can only imitate and pervert what God has already created. In the context of marine demons, God created the water for His purposes.

In Genesis 1:20-22, God says, *"Let the waters teem with swarms of living creatures.... God created the great sea monsters and every living creature that moves, with which the waters swarmed after their kind.... God blessed them, saying, 'Be fruitful and multiply, and fill the waters in the seas....'"*

Satan and his cohorts seek to pollute and pervert those purposes. There are startling parallels to this truth in the natural realm. Water pollution is a growing problem around the world. According to the Borgen Project,[3] "personal care products and pharmaceuticals, including birth control pills, antibiotics and painkillers, are washed into water reservoirs and lakes, contributing to the rising water pollution. They have a damaging effect on the aquatic ecosystems and cause hormonal imbalances in humans and animals."

Borgen also reports approximately 946 million people are forced to defecate in street gutters and near water bodies, exacerbating the rising water pollution and 1.8 million people rely on drinking water potentially contaminated by human waste. Contaminated drinking water and inadequate sanitation cause more deaths annually than violence from the ongoing wars. Approximately 842,000 people, including 361,000 children under five, die yearly from diarrhea.

DoSomething.org reports[4] the Mississippi River carries an estimated 1.5 million metric tons of nitrogen pollution into the Gulf of Mexico each year, creating a "dead zone" in the Gulf each summer about the size of New Jersey. And approximately 40 percent of the lakes in the United States of America are too polluted for fishing, aquatic life, or swimming.

And *Ocean Health* reports[5] the Pacific Ocean is turning into a desert: "The waters of the Pacific off the coast of California are a clear, shimmering blue today, so transparent it's possible to see the sandy bottom below [...] clear water is a sign that the ocean is turning into a desert, and the chain reaction that causes that bitter clarity is perhaps most obvious on the beaches of the Golden State, where thousands of emaciated sea lion pups are stranded."

Indeed, the enemy is manifesting his ministry to kill, steal, and destroy (see John 10:10) by polluting the waters with marine demons. It seems in many cases the water is bitter and there's poison in the pot. We see these concepts in Scripture.

After the Israelites left Egypt, they came to Marah but could not drink the waters because they were bitter. Moses cried out to the Lord, and He told the prophet to throw a tree into the water to make the water sweet (see Exodus 15:23-24). Elisha came across poisoned water and purified it with salt (see 2 Kings 2:19-22). All of this is a manifestation of what is happening in the unseen spirit realm—demons are influencing spiritual climates and natural waters.

How Marine Demons Influence People

Great cities of the world surrounded by water or home to large bodies of water see the influence of marine demons on their communities—and the people who live in them. From witchcraft to greed to murder, we see historical and present-day manifestations of water spirits all around the world, but especially in marked by significant rivers, seas, bays, channels, wetlands, and swamps.

An article in *Port Strategy*[6] magazine waxes prophetic in the world of water spirits. The magazine reports the US government is working to reclaim the docks from the mob and has filed a legal case against organized crime bosses. The American mafia's corruption on the waterfront dates back to the

1930s. The mafia's strategy to dominate the ports is demonic masterminding at its best.

With a stronghold in the ports, the mafia infiltrated the US economy, working in gambling, gas-tax fraud, restaurants, and racketeering in many industries. Rituals, rules, and customs emerged, as well as symbolism in violent acts and murder. Of course, the mafia was birthed in Sicily, Italy, which is home to seas and channels where marine demons thrive. Could it be possible marine demons defiled the hearts of businessmen who could have used their ambition for godly kingdom exploits?

College students from around the world flock to beach cities, like Panama City, Florida,[7] for Spring Break each year. The parties are marked by sexual immorality, drugs, drunkenness, psychic readings. Gang rapes have been reported on crowded beaches, as well as house party shootings, binge drinking, sexual perversion, robberies, and more are common during Spring Breaks. Could it be possible these good kids go buck wild in an atmosphere driven by marine demon agendas?

Likewise, the top states in the US for human trafficking are water cities. According to Human Trafficking Search,[8] California, Texas, Florida, and New York are the top four states for this wicked practice. Could it be possible that marine demons have built territorial strongholds that pave the way for horrifying human trafficking strategies?

Like the US government that's filing a legal case against the mafia,[9] Christians need to legislate in the courts of Heaven against marine demons that are influencing their cities. Much the same, individuals need to take personal responsibility to identify the temptations and influences marine demons introduce to their souls—from pride to rebellion to sexual immorality and beyond—and resist it. Of course, apart from Christ it's difficult to resist evil, which is why marine demons oppose the Gospel in the territories over which they have erected dominions and thrones.

Endnotes

1. *USGS*, "How much water is there on, in, and above the Earth?"; https://water.usgs.gov/edu/earthhowmuch.html; accessed April 18, 2018.

2. *USGS*, "The water in you"; https://water.usgs.gov/edu/propertyyou.html; accessed April 18, 2018.

3. *The Borgen Project*, "10 Facts About Water Pollution," April 2017; https://borgenproject.org/10-facts-about-water-pollution/; accessed April 18, 2018.

4. *DoSsometing.org*, "11 Facts About Pollution," https://www.dosomething.org/us/facts/11-facts-about-pollution; accessed April 18, 2018.

5. Mac Slavo, *GlobalResearch*, May 2015 "'The Ocean is Dying': Marine and Animal Life Die Offs, California Coast" https://www.globalresearch.ca/the-ocean-is-dying-marine-and-animal-life-die-offs-california-coast/5451836; accessed April 18, 2018.

6. *PortStrategy*, "US Government Takes on Waterfront Mafia," September 1, 2005; http://www.portstrategy.com/news101/world/americas/us_government_takes_on_waterfront_mafia; accessed April 18, 2018.

7. John Murgatroyd, *CNN*, "Panama City gang rape: 'Spring break as we know it is over,'" April 16, 2015; http://www.cnn.com/2015/04/15/us/florida-panama-city-beach-spring-break/index.html; accessed April 18, 2018.

8. HumanTraffickingSearch, "Top 4 States for Human Trafficking," posted by Sarah Pierce, 2014; http://humantraffickingsearch.org/top-4-states-for-human-trafficking/; accessed April 18, 2018.

9. The Federal Bureau of Investigation, "On the Waterfront, Mafia-Style," December 16, 2008; https://archives.fbi.gov/archives/news/stories/2008/december/unirac_121608; accessed April 18, 2018.

Chapter 2

THE ORIGIN
OF MARINE DEMONS

W HEN I was a secular journalist, I went on assignment to the Dry
Tortugas National Park off the shores of the Florida Keys. Home
to the largest marine sanctuary of its kind in the United States,
the area is off limits to fishing to preserve highly exploited marine life species.
I had a front-row view of magnificent coral and exotic fish as the sun beat
down on the boat deck. What I couldn't see were the marine demons below
the surface.

The oceans and waters of the earth are filled with beautiful creatures—and
some of them are dangerous. Take the Striped Surgeonfish as a natural example. With its nearly neon green and blue stripes, this fish is stunning—but
its spine is venomous. Hideous marine demons are trolling below the surface
of the water with a deadly agenda to kill, steal, and destroy lives. You can't
see them any more than you can see spirits of fear or rejection, but they are
actively engaged in aquatic ministry.

Perhaps the closest parallel we can make between natural sea creatures
and marine demons are the jellyfish. Some jellyfish merely sting—others
are deadly like the Sea Wasp Box Jellyfish (the deadliest in the world), the

Portuguese Man O' War (which is technically a colony of organisms) and the Irukandji Jellyfish. According to Conservation Institute,[1] you're unlikely to see this tiny creature coming because it's only 0.02 inches and is nearly transparent. The Conservation Institute writes:

> It is a member of the notorious box jellyfish family, and is arguably the most venomous animal on the planet. Its toxin is 100 stronger than that of a cobra. Both the tentacles and bell can sting. A single sting may be treatable. Multiple stings are almost certainly deadly. Symptoms include severe muscle cramps, pain in the kidneys and back, burning sensations, headache, vomiting, and tachycardia. If you live, it won't be a fun memory.

Marine demons are like venomous jellyfish. They release toxic imaginations as they work to wrap their tentacles around you. The attack can sting your soul or body. If you don't discern the attack quickly enough and sustain multiple stings, it could kill relationships, steal your peace of mind or health, and destroy opportunities God has planned for you. You can defeat it. The battle won't be a fun memory but the victory will be sweet.

Warfare in Three Heavenly Realms

There are three realms of the universe: the heavenlies, the earth, and the sea. Psalm 146:6 (NKJV) tells us God made the *"heaven and earth, the sea, and all that is in them."* Here we see three realms of creation—and three realms of spiritual strongholds. In Nehemiah 9:6, the Levites said, *"You alone are the Lord. You have made the heavens, the heaven of heavens with all their host, the earth and all that is on it, the seas and all that is in them...."* The Bible speaks of the heavenly host, which are the angels who make their abode in heaven (see Deuteronomy 17:3). And Jesus spoke repeatedly of our heavenly Father.

The Bible speaks of heavenly things (see John 3:12), heavenly visions (see Acts 26:19), heavenly bodies (see 1 Corinthians 15:40), heavenly places (see Ephesians 1:3), a heavenly Kingdom (see 2 Timothy 4:18), our heavenly calling (see Hebrews 3:1), the heavenly gift (see Hebrews 6:4), and the heavenly Jerusalem (see Hebrews 12:22). All of this speaks to the Heaven where Jesus sits at the right hand of the Father and is part of the heavenlies. We know this as the third heaven.

Paul's words in 2 Corinthians 12:2-4 suggest three heavens:

> *I know a man in Christ who fourteen years ago—whether in the body I do not know, or out of the body I do not know, God knows—such a man was caught up to the third heaven. And I know how such a man—whether in the body or apart from the body I do not know, God knows—was caught up into Paradise and heard inexpressible words, which a man is not permitted to speak.*

Common sense informs us if there is a third heaven, there must be a second heaven and a first heaven. The concept of the second heaven is found in Revelation 8:13: *"Then I looked, and I heard an eagle flying in midheaven, saying with a loud voice, 'Woe, woe, woe to those who dwell on the earth, because of the remaining blasts of the trumpet of the three angels who are about to sound!'"*

We see supernatural activity in the midheaven, or second heaven, with other references found in Revelation 14:6 and Revelation 19:17. Spiritual conflicts take place in the second heaven. When the Prince of Persia withstood the angel seeking to deliver Daniel's prayer answers, this skirmish took place in the midheaven. Much of the spiritual warfare with which we are familiar is taking place in the second heaven. The first heaven is the atmosphere around us. It includes the clouds, the moon, the sun, and the stars.

However, the enemy is roaming the earth like a roaring lion seeking someone to devour (see 1 Peter 5:8). We see confirmation of this in Job 1:6-7,

"Now there was a day when the sons of God came to present themselves before the Lord, and Satan also came among them. The Lord said to Satan, 'From where do you come?' Then Satan answered the Lord and said, 'From roaming about on the earth and walking around on it.'"

Most of the warfare we deal with in the first heaven is the battle against our mind. Satan is the god of this world (see 2 Corinthians 4:4) and influences the hearts and minds of people—even those who know the Lord. Satan filled Judas' heart to betray Jesus (see Luke 22:3) and Ananias' heart to lie to the Holy Spirit about his giving (see Acts 5:3). The Pharisees were influenced to reject Jesus at His first coming (see John 8:44). Peter was influenced by demonic thoughts to rebuke Jesus (see Matthew 16:22-23). The tempter tempts us to sin through exploiting our fleshly appetites and whispering vain imaginations to our soul (see 2 Corinthians 10:5).

The third realm or stronghold of creation is the seas. In Exodus 20:4, the Lord speaks expressly: *"You shall not make for yourself an idol, or any likeness of what is in heaven above or on the earth beneath or in the water under the earth."* Many Christians have never heard of water spirits but the Bible speaks of the category of sea monsters—on many occasions. Ancient religions have made gods of sea creatures, but these are really demonic entities.

A few of the Scriptures that mention water spirits include: Ezekiel 29:3-4, Job 3, Revelation 17:1-2, Revelation 12:12, and 1 Samuel 5:3. Acts 6 mentions the Python Spirit. Isaiah 27:1 mentions Leviathan. While some of these verses speak to specific marine demons and the principles of defeating them, others offer evidence to the broader classification of water spirits—or how spirits work in the waters.

Revelation 12:12 is perhaps the best example: *"For this reason, rejoice, O heavens and you who dwell in them. Woe to the earth and the sea, because the devil has come down to you, having great wrath, knowing that he has only a short time."*

Most spiritual warriors are quick to quote 1 Peter 5:8, which tells us the enemy is roaming about like a roaring lion seeking to devour believers. We relegate the devil to the earth realm or the second heaven. But Revelation 12:12 clearly connects the devil to the oceanic realm. You could rightly say the enemy is roaming around like a sea monster seeking to devour and it would be an accurate representation of marine demons.

It's interesting to note that when all things are made new after the Second Coming of Christ, the sea—which makes up over 70 percent of the earth's surface—is nowhere to be found. Revelation 21:1 (NKJV) makes it plain: *"Now I saw a new heaven and a new earth, for the first heaven and the first earth had passed away. Also there was no more sea."*

Was the Earth Once Covered With Water?

Scripture is clear—before the earth had land it was covered with water (see Genesis 1:2). You might say, in the beginning God created the heavens and earth, which was void of land. The Smithsonian claims water came to earth as part of the Big Bang nearly 14 billion years ago.[2] The Big Bang Theory is the evolutionist's explanation of how the earth began, defying God as Creator.

NASA explains that, "In 1927, an astronomer named Georges Lemaître had a big idea. He said that a very long time ago, the universe started as just a single point. He said the universe stretched and expanded to get as big as it is now, and that it could keep on stretching." The Smithsonian imagines a complicated story line in which stars enter the picture and bring oxygen to combine with the hydrogen carried in particles from the Big Bang.[3]

That's more difficult to believe than an invisible God with power to create heavens and earth. Again, Scripture is clear. Beyond Genesis 1:2, Genesis 1:9-10 (NKJV) tells us, *"Then God said, 'Let the waters below the heavens be gathered into one place, and let the dry land appear'; and it was so. God called the dry land earth, and the gathering of the waters He called seas; and God saw that it was good."*

In this account, we conclude that water is foundational to life. That's why when scientists research the possibility of life on other planets, they search for the presence of water. In fact, NASA's mantra in the hunt for extraterrestrial life has been "follow the water."[4] Adam and Eve could not have lived on an earth without water. Water was a prerequisite of life.

Will God Judge the Seas?

Revelation 21:1 is fascinating. Could the absence of the sea be part of God's judgment on marine demons that proliferate in the world's oceans? Some theologians believe so. R.C. Sproul points out what may to some be a contrary reality in the new earth. Many enjoy the seas during vacations. They find the sea's beauty relaxing. Indeed, waterfront properties carry more value per square foot than real estate in the farmlands of America because of the scarcity of coastal land. However, he explains:

> In Jewish literature, the sea was often used as a symbol for that which was ominous, sinister, and threatening. Earlier in the Revelation of John, we see the Beast emerging from the sea (Rev. 13). Likewise, in ancient Semitic mythology, there is frequent reference to the primordial sea monster that represents the shadowy chaos. The Babylonian goddess Tiamat is a case in point.[5]

Remember when Jesus walked on water? The disciples' reaction was telling of how Jews viewed the spiritual atmosphere of the sea:

> *Immediately He made the disciples get into the boat and go ahead of Him to the other side, while He sent the crowds away. After He had sent the crowds away, He went up on the mountain by Himself to pray; and when it was evening, He was there alone. But the boat was already a long distance from the*

> *land, battered by the waves; for the wind was contrary. And in*
> *the fourth watch of the night He came to them, walking on the*
> *sea. When the disciples saw Him walking on the sea, they were*
> *terrified, and said, "It is a ghost!" And they cried out in fear.*
> *But immediately Jesus spoke to them, saying, "Take courage, it*
> *is I; do not be afraid"* (Matthew 14:22-27).

Immediately, the disciples concluded they were seeing a ghost. Other translations use the word spirit, illusion, or apparition. They may have thought that the ghost was the impetus behind the storm. The Greek word for "ghost" in that verse is *phantasma,* which means an appearance, an apparition of a spectre. It only appears twice in Scripture—and the other reference is the parallel account of Jesus walking on water in Mark 6:49—but it says plenty about the Jewish mindset about the ominous nature of the seas.

All that said, it's likely that the "no more sea" passage is more symbolic than literal. G.K. Beale in *The Book of Revelation: A Commentary on the Greek Text,* concludes, "In all likelihood, 'sea' is figurative for old-world threats. Therefore, the presence of a literal sea in the new creation would not be inconsistent with the figurative exclusion of the sea in 21:1."

Old-world threats would include marine demons. As we end this study, it's worth looking at another sea mentioned in the Book of Revelation. The sea(s) of glass is mentioned twice—Revelation 4:6 and Revelation 15:2. Speaking of God's throne, John wrote, *"Before the throne there was something like a sea of glass, like crystal"* (Revelation 4:6). And again, John *"saw something like a sea of glass mixed with fire, and those who had been victorious over the beast and his image and the number of his name, standing on the sea of glass, holding harps of God"* (Revelation 15:2).

When you translate the Greek, John saw what appeared to be a transparent or glassy body of water around God's throne. Various Bible commentators offer diverse explanations of what this actually means—from an actual sea to a reflection of God's glory to the Word of God in a physical representation.

What we know for sure is this sea is pure, holy, and undefiled. The seas of glass in the new earth will be free from all pollution, perversion, and defilement. God's new sea will serve as one more platform to worship the Creator of the new heaven and new earth.

Endnotes

1. Conservation Institute, "7 Most Deadliest, Most Poisonous Jellyfish in the World," April 24, 2014; http://www.conservationinstitute. org/7-deadliest-poisonous-jellyfish-world/; accessed April 18, 2018.

2. Brian Greene, "How Did Water Come to Earth?" *Smithsonian Magazine,* May 2013; https://www.smithsonianmag.com/science-nature/ how-did-water-come-to-earth-72037248/; accessed April 18, 2018.

3. NASA Space Place, "What is the Big Bang?" https://spaceplace.nasa. gov/big-bang/en/; accessed April 18, 2018.

4. NASA Fact Sheet, "Follow the Water—Finding a Perfect Match for Life," April 16, 2007; https://www.nasa.gov/vision/earth/everydaylife/ jamestown-water-fs.html; accessed April 18, 2018.

5. R.C. Sproul, "There Will Be No Sea in the New Heaven and New Earth," Ligonier Ministries, August 18, 2014; http://www.ligonier.org/ blog/there-will-be-no-sea-new-heaven-and-new-earth/; accessed April 18, 2018.

Chapter 3

WHAT MAKES

WATER SPIRITS SO POWERFUL?

WHILE writing the first two chapters of this book, I took one of the hardest spiritual warfare hits of my life—and I'm no battlefield novice. It seemed to come out of absolutely nowhere, but it was a high-level tactical plan against my destiny.

I woke up on Sunday morning feeling stiff in my body, with a whopping migraine headache. My state of mind could best be described as a scrambled egg. I could not string together two thoughts because the vain imaginations were hitting my mind in rapid-fire succession. Before I could cast one down, another took its place. It's as if the demon powers were competing with one another as to who could deliver the knockout punch.

The overarching emotion that worked to overwhelm my soul was defeat, then disgust, the desperation for breakthrough. My chest grew tight. I had a difficult time breathing. My heart started pounding. I stood. I paced. I sat. I warred. I praised. I called for intercessory prayer backup. I did everything I'd been taught to do, but dizziness gripped my head and I felt like no oxygen was getting to my brain.

Somehow, in my determination I made it to church but I had no idea how I was going to preach the Word. In the back office, I started chocking. I was not overcome, but I was dazed and confused. I was never once afraid, but I was angry. At one point, I felt powerless to break through the attack. Thank God, I had an intercessor standing with me who went in deep.

I had never experienced anything like it before and hope never to again—it was just that intense. As my intercessor prayed, she began shaking with righteous indignation. I literally felt the enemy loose my body and my mind.

When I say literally, I mean literally. One moment I was in physical and mental distress. The next minute I was free and clear and felt completely normal. Yes, just like that. I am still learning from the experience, though I am certain several water spirits formed a confederate to attack me—backlash from exposing this wicked demonic underbelly.

What Makes Water Spirits So Powerful?

After the attack I just described, I gained an even deeper determination to answer the question posted as the chapter title: What Makes Water Spirits So Powerful? I've battled many spirits in my day and never sustained such an attack as the one just described. Was it my ignorance of the depth of depravity among these spirits? Was I ill-prepared for the backlash I'd get in the midst of writing this book to set captives free from marine demon grips? Or is there some other reason? This attack was especially difficult, albeit definitely not impossible, to defeat. Why?

Battling marine demons is not our ordinary warfare. I believe the primary reason water spirits seem so powerful—even though they are actually no more powerful than any other demon and certainly nowhere near as powerful as the Spirit that raised Christ from the dead that dwells in us (see Romans 8:11)—I believe our ignorance has given marine demons what seems like an upper hand in battle. Let's review what the Bible says about ignorance and knowledge.

Marine demons roam undetected, making as little sound as possible until they are close enough to strike.

The Biggest Danger Is Lacking Discernment

The biggest danger for a submarine is radar. Marine demons have fallen below or failed to register on the radar screens of most of the church. We are ignorant of marine demons and therefore fail to discern their operations against our lives. Like a submarine with a radar reflector, marine demons divert attention to other demons so we can't see them.

Throughout the course of this book, we'll learn a spiritual form of anti-submarine warfare. In 1969, *Popular Mechanics* defined anti-submarine warfare, or ASW, as detecting, tracking, and destroying a maneuvering target that can't be seen.[4] Your success in defeating marine demon attacks depends on discernment, training, and experience.

If you've ever wrestled with a marine demon, you've had hands-on training and experience that was probably as frightening as Navy Seal training. The attack I mentioned at the start of this chapter reminds me of one of the exercises Seals endure: Trainees are thrown into the water with heavy weights fastened to their feet. They have to hold their breath while an instructor rips and tears apart their air tank. The trainee is tasked with putting the air tank back together before he runs out of air, then swimming back up to fresh air while the instructor harasses them.[5] The good news is—God is the air we breathe.

Beyond the Navy Seals, there are the Army's elite combat divers. Part of the training is called "drown-proofing." This is a method for surviving in water disaster scenarios without sinking or drowning.

Here's how the training works: The combat divers are tied up, thrown into the water and left to do various maneuvers to gain air. One of the maneuvers is to exhale and sink, crouch and bounce back up, and inhale at the top of the water. Another is to bend their knees in a floating position at the surface of the water, then kick their feet back to raise up above the water to inhale.[6] The key to drown-proofing, ultimately, is to take deep breaths and stay calm. Likewise, in underwater warfare, we must breathe deep from and stay calm.

God Has Ultimate Dominion Over the Waters

The good news is God created the waters and has ultimate dominion over the water. Consider Psalm 104:5-9:

> *He [God] established the earth upon its foundations, so that it will not totter forever and ever. You covered it with the deep as with a garment; the waters were standing above the mountains. At Your rebuke they fled, at the sound of Your thunder they hurried away. The mountains rose; the valleys sank down to the place which You established for them. You set a boundary that they may not pass over, so that they will not return to cover the earth.*

God parted the Red Sea (see Exodus 14:15-31). God parted the Jordan River (see Joshua 4:23). Jesus walked on the sea (see Matthew 14:25). Jesus commanded the sea to be still (see Mark 4:39). God keeps the sea inside its boundaries so the water will not cover the earth (see Job 38:8; Psalm 33:7; 104:9; Proverbs 8:29; Jeremiah 5:22). God rules the swelling of the sea (see Psalm 89:9). He sent a whale to pick up a prophet in the sea (see Jonah 1:15). The voice of the Lord is upon the waters—the Lord is over many waters (see Psalm 29:3).

First Samuel 5:3-5 demonstrates how water spirits cannot stand against Jehovah:

> *When the Ashdodites arose early the next morning, behold, Dagon had fallen on his face to the ground before the ark of*

the Lord. So they took Dagon and set him in his place again. But when they arose early the next morning, behold, Dagon had fallen on his face to the ground before the ark of the Lord. And the head of Dagon and both the palms of his hands were cut off on the threshold; only the trunk of Dagon was left to him. Therefore neither the priests of Dagon nor all who enter Dagon's house tread on the threshold of Dagon in Ashdod to this day.

God gave us dominion not only over the earth, but also over the sea—He gave humankind dominion. God said, *"Let Us make man in Our image, according to Our likeness; and let them rule over the fish of the sea and over the birds of the sky and over the cattle and over all the earth, and over every creeping thing that creeps on the earth"* (Genesis 1:26). Marine demons have to bow to the name of Jesus just like any other demon.

Genesis 9:2 further explains our dominion over water spirits: *"The fear of you and the terror of you will be on every beast of the earth and on every bird of the sky; with everything that creeps on the ground, and all the fish of the sea, into your hand they are given."*

Ephesians 1:22 tells us God placed all things under Christ's feet. We are Christ's Body, which means all things are under our feet—including water spirits. Psalm 8:6-8 affirms, *"You make him to rule over the works of Your hands; You have put all things under his feet, all sheep and oxen, and also the beasts of the field, the birds of the heavens and the fish of the sea, whatever passes through the paths of the seas."*

Luke 10:19-20 alludes to the manifestation of water spirits, given a Python spirit is part of the snake family. Jesus said, *"Behold, I have given you authority to tread on serpents and scorpions, and over all the power of the enemy, and nothing will injure you. Nevertheless do not rejoice in this, that the spirits are subject to you, but rejoice that your names are recorded in heaven."* Water spirits are subject to you.

Angels Can Help You
in the War Against Water Spirits

The Bible also speaks of the angel of the water in Revelation 16:5, which makes it clear the heavenly host is available to help us do battle in this stronghold. What is the angel of the water? Ellicott's Commentary for English Readers reveals this is "the angel who was set over the waters, or the angel who is, on the heavenly side, representative of the water. The angel acknowledges God's righteousness."

Barnes's Notes on the Bible explains this is "the angel who presides over the element of water." This angel is, according to *Gill's Exposition of the Entire Bible,* "'the prince of the sea,' and of the angels that were over the waters...." And *Pulpit Commentary* shares this angel's duty is to "control the rivers." It's not a stretch to believe this angel would dispatch other angels to war in the waters for God's will.

As I wrote in my book, *Angels on Assignment Again,* God sends angels on an assignment to fight for His people in times of war. In the Old Testament, we see examples of this in the physical realm. In the New Testament—in the Book of Revelation—we see a war in the heavens. Listen in to this startling account in 2 Kings 19:34-35:

> *"For I will defend this city to save it for My own sake and for My servant David's sake." Then it happened that night that the angel of the Lord went out and struck 185,000 in the camp of the Assyrians; and when men rose early in the morning, behold, all of them were dead.*

As mighty as David was in battle—after all he defeated Goliath with a sling and a stone when the rest of the children of Israel were shaking in their boots and sang songs about how he slew tens of thousands (see 1 Samuel 18:7)—he still called on angels of war in times of distress. David prayed to the

Lord to send angels on assignment to fight for him in war in Psalm 35. You'll notice how David depends on the Lord, but calls for the angels.

> *Plead my cause, O Lord, with those who strive with me; fight against those who fight against me. Take hold of shield and buckler, and stand up for my help. Also draw out the spear, and stop those who pursue me. Say to my soul, "I am your salvation." Let those be put to shame and brought to dishonor who seek after my life; let those be turned back and brought to confusion who plot my hurt. Let them be like chaff before the wind, and let the angel of the Lord chase them. Let their way be dark and slippery,*
>
> *and let the angel of the Lord pursue them. For without cause they have hidden their net for me in a pit, which they have dug without cause for my life* (Psalm 35:1-7 NKJV).

Jesus Himself mentioned angels in the context of war on the night of His betrayal in the Garden of Gethsemane. Peter's first response to the soldiers trying to take Jesus into custody was to pull out his sword and fight. But Jesus corrected him in Matthew 26:52-54:

> *Then Jesus said to him, "Put your sword back in its place. For all those who take up the sword will perish by the sword. Do you think that I cannot appeal to My Father, and He will at once put at My disposal more than twelve legions of angels? How then will the Scriptures be fulfilled, which say that it must happen this way?"*

In the Book of Revelation, we read about an epic war between good and evil—a battle between the archangel Michael and his angels and a cohort of demons. The dramatic account is recorded in Revelation 12:6-8 (NKJV), demonstrating the warring nature of some angels on assignment.

> *Then the woman fled into the wilderness, where she has a place prepared by God, that they should feed her there one thousand two hundred and sixty days. And war broke out in heaven: Michael and his angels fought with the dragon; and the dragon and his angels fought, but they did not prevail, nor was a place found for them in heaven any longer.*

Through the pages of this chapter, you've seen why marine demons seem so powerful—but you've also seen your authority to defeat them and the heavenly host at your disposal to fight this good fight of faith.

Endnotes

1. https://www.navy.com/careers/special-operations/seals.html#ft-key-responsibilities; accessed April 18, 2018.

2. Armin Rosen, "Sweden Is Learning Just How Insanely Difficult It Is To Capture An Enemy Submarine," Business Insider, October 22, 2014; http://www.businessinsider.com/capturing-a-submarine-is-insanely-difficult-2014-10; accessed April 18, 2018.

3. "Why are stealth submarines so difficult to find?" http://www.dw.com/en/why-are-stealth-submarines-so-difficult-to-find/a-41489445; accessed April 18, 2018.

4. Bob Zimmerman, "Antisubmarine Warfare," *Popular Mechanics,* September 1969; https://books.google.com/books?id=M9gDAAAAM-BAJ&pg=PA114#v=onepage&q&f=false; accessed April 18, 2018.

5. Luke Kerr-Dineen, "This insane underwater training exercise proves Navy SEALs are actual superheroes," USATODAY, January 5, 2017;

http://ftw.usatoday.com/2017/01/this-insane-underwater-training-exercise-proves-navy-seals-are-actual-superheroes; accessed April 18, 2018.

6. Clint Emerson, "A retired Navy SEAL explains how to survive a drowning attempt," *Business Insider,* December 17, 2015; http://www.businessinsider.com/navy-seal-explains-how-to-survive-a-drowning-attempt-2015-12; accessed April 18, 2018.

Chapter 4

PYTHON
SPIRIT'S PRESSURE

L UWALA was born to a spirit named Mbirimu, a shapeshifter who could take on the form of a human or an animal, according to a legend often told in Uganda's Lake Victoria. When Mbirimu grew lonely, he morphed into a woman and birthed twin brothers—one was a python and the other a human.

Luwala was the python. His twin brother built a shrine for him and the Abassesse tribe, remembered as a race of super humans, worshipped the python. Luwala's brother became a priest to the python and operated in healing powers, according to a BBC report.[1]

The line of healers Mbirimu supposedly birthed is still operating in Uganda in the 21st century—and so is the Python spirit. Essentially, it's a spirit of divination. Divination is the "art or practice that seeks to foresee or foretell future events or discover hidden knowledge usually by the interpretation of omens or by the aid of supernatural powers," according to *Merriam-Webster*. The problem is, diviners tap into the spirit illegally and serve up false signs and wonders.

In Uganda's culture, the line of healers the Python spirit empowers are called *emandwa*. *The BBC's* Amy Gigi Alexander explains *emandwa* means "*the* man who has a spirit sit on his head" and that the traditional healer is the only person who can speak to Luwala, and it's through him that all requests are made. As Alexander tells it, the *emandwa* is charged with keeping a fire burning 24/7 to please the python spirit. Inside the python's hut are bowls that contain offerings to the spirit, which promises the hope of fertility, wealth, protection, and more.

Although we see variations of Python worship in various cultures—indeed this is an ancient principality that has infiltrated the nations with different storylines—this spirit is rooted in Greco-Roman mythology. The Python spirit is even mentioned in the Bible. In fact, it's one of the few spirits the Bible actually names specifically. Before we explore what the Bible says about Python, it's helpful to understand the mythology behind it.

Mythology is considered an allegorical narrative that explains the exploits of gods, demigods, and legendary heroes; but as I mentioned in our opening chapter, the ancients created these storylines to articulate supernatural powers in the unseen realm that worked in their cultures. Myths, in other words, simply worked to describe in natural words the activity of demon spirits whose operations manifested in the natural.

Encyclopedia Britannica reveals:

> Python, in Greek mythology, a huge serpent that was killed by the god Apollo at Delphi either because it would not let him found his oracle, being accustomed itself to giving oracles, or because it had persecuted Apollo's mother, Leto, during her pregnancy. In the earliest account, the Homeric Hymn to Apollo, the serpent is nameless and female, but later it is male, as in Euripides' Iphigenia Among the Taurians, and named Python (found first in the account of the 4th-century-BC historian Ephorus; Pytho was the old

name for Delphi). Python was traditionally the child of Gaea (Earth) who had an oracle at Delphi before Apollo came. The Pythian Games held at Delphi were supposed to have been instituted by Apollo to celebrate his victory over Python.[2]

Python's Predatory Purpose

Python's ultimate purpose is to cut off your lifeline to God—to keep you from praying to your heavenly Father, to stop you from hearing the Holy Spirit's voice, and to hinder your fellowship with the Jesus. Think about it for a minute. Prayer is how we communicate with God—and the concept is mentioned over 250 times in Scripture.

Prayer is not something we do in desperate times only; prayer is how we sustain our relationship with the Lord. There are many different kinds of prayer. The prayer of faith is released to heal the sick (see James 5:15). The prayer of consecration sets you apart for God's purposes (see Acts 13:2). The prayer of worship is when we exalt God. The prayer of commitment is when we cast our cares upon Him (1 Peter 5:7). The prayer in the spirit is when we speak mysteries to God (see 1 Corinthians 14:2) and build ourselves up in our most holy faith (Jude 20). The prayer of binding and loosing is part of our spiritual warfare arsenal (see Matthew 18:18-19).

Prayer is critical to living a victorious life in Christ. Prayer is the main vehicle of how God responds to our needs and our desires. Prayer is how God prophesied to us about our future, offers words of wisdom about our past, words of knowledge about our present, and releases the spirit of counsel. Prayer is how we repent of our sins and find strength to stand and withstand in the trials of life and the spiritual warfare we face. Prayer is how we bring godly change into our families, workplaces, schools, and cities. Prayer demonstrates our reliance on God.

Python knows if it can choke out our prayer life, it can go in for the kill. Python understands that if we can't pray, we will never see our dreams in Christ come alive. Python knows if it can suffocate our prayer life, our impact will be minimized, if not neutralized. Python will prophesy lies to your soul to woo you into a web of witchcraft that makes you feel weary. Python pressures you out of your passion. Python overwhelms you with hopelessness.

Paul's Encounter with Python

Paul the apostle encountered the Python spirit on his missionary journeys. The Holy Spirit saw it fit to chronicle this encounter by the hand of Luke, who penned the Book of Acts. We read about the showdown in Acts 16:16-18:

> *It happened that as we were going to the place of prayer, a slave-girl having a spirit of divination met us, who was bringing her masters much profit by fortune-telling. Following after Paul and us, she kept crying out, saying, "These men are bond-servants of the Most High God, who are proclaiming to you the way of salvation." She continued doing this for many days. But Paul was greatly annoyed, and turned and said to the spirit, "I command you in the name of Jesus Christ to come out of her!" And it came out at that very moment.*

The Greek word for "divination" in that verse is *puthon*. The *KJV New Testament Greek Lexicon* defines it this way: "In Greek mythology the name of the Pythian serpent or dragon that dwelt in the region of Pytho at the foot of Parnassus in Phocis, and was said to have guarded the oracle at Delphi and been slain by Apollo; a spirit of divination." This is in line with Greek mythology, but clearly Python is more than a myth since Paul cast the spirit out of the girl.

Python, which is a principality, releases witchcraft, which is a power in the Ephesians 6:12 hierarchy. The Python spirit is a coiling spirit that works to squeeze out the breath of life (the Holy Spirit) and cut off your lifeline to God (prayer). Symptoms of a Python attack may include weariness, a loss of passion to worship and pray, feeling pressured, overwhelmed, helpless, and even hopeless. The severity of those symptoms depends on how long this enemy has been coiling itself around you and how much pressure it has applied.

Python can attack anyone. As with any other spiritual attack, you don't have to be in sin to find python trying to slide under your door. Paul was a man of prayer. The Bible says he spoke in tongues more than anybody else in the Corinthian church (1 Corinthians 14:18)—and probably more than anybody else in the early church.

Despite Paul's relationship with Christ and a strong prayer life, he still had to wrestle against principalities and powers and rulers of the darkness of this age and spiritual hosts of wickedness in the heavenly places (see Ephesians 6:12). Paul had to wrestle against Python—and so may we. Let's look at Paul's encounter with the Python spirit.

The Python spirit had a stronghold in Philippi. When the man of prayer started heading for the house of prayer, this spirit launched its first attack against him—a distraction followed by a full-blown trial that aimed to take him out of his purpose. Python knows it has no authority in a city that prays in the presence of God, so it works to distract people from praying so they can't fulfill their purpose.

Python would rather watch you lick your wounds than pray to a healing God. Python would rather hear you complain or gossip than take your problems to a miracle-working God. Python would rather distract you with attacks, trials, and persecutions than see you press into a gracious God for deliverance. Again, Python's ultimate goal is to put you in bondage and thwart your purpose. You may be going through the motions but you feel dead on the inside because Python has squeezed the life out of you.

When you rise up in your Christ-given authority against Python, the battle ensues. Paul cast the demon out of the girl, which meant her masters could no longer profit from her false prophecies. Acts 16:19-24 reveals:

> *But when her masters saw that their hope of profit was gone, they seized Paul and Silas and dragged them into the market place before the authorities, and when they had brought them to the chief magistrates, they said, "These men are throwing our city into confusion, being Jews, and are proclaiming customs which it is not lawful for us to accept or to observe, being Romans." The crowd rose up together against them, and the chief magistrates tore their robes off them and proceeded to order them to be beaten with rods. When they had struck them with many blows, they threw them into prison, commanding the jailer to guard them securely; and he, having received such a command, threw them into the inner prison and fastened their feet in the stocks.*

In this passage, we see several Python tactics: false accusations, violent persecution, and ultimately bondage. The Python spirit seeks to inflict wounds on you with accusations and spiritual blows to your body. This spirit will also work through hurts and wounds of your past, magnifying unresolved pain to stop or hinder your prayer life and stop you from accomplishing your God-given mission.

How Pythons Attack

In the wetlands and the waters, Pythons attack in several ways. One of the most common and the master technique is by coiling themselves around their victims. According to *National Geographic*, pythons strike at you and grab you with their teeth: "They'll seize the prey item with their teeth and simultaneously wrap their coil around it and squeeze. And when the victim inhales, that's the time they squeeze a little bit harder to the point where you can't really get a breath anymore."[3]

Translating this to the realm of the spirit, Pythons attack in the midst of turmoil. As opportunistic hunters, they often strike in the midst of drama when you most need to pray. *Merriam-Webster* defines toil as "turmoil" and "trouble; also: everyday cares and worries." When we carry our mortal coil, as William Shakespeare would say—when we carry our cares instead of casting them on the Lord according to 1 Peter 5:7—we are giving opportunity to this ambush predator to strike while we're weak and distracted.

Of course, that's not the only time Python strikes. You could be walking in perfect peace on your mission in God and, like Paul and Silas, get blindsided from behind. Python snakes, ultimately, put pressure on your heart. Scientists have concluded the heart goes into cardiac arrest before the oxygen runs out. In other words, Pythons are cutting off the blood supply that results in a heart attack.[4]

Python spirits are attacking your heart—your lifeline to God through the blood. When Python attacks, you might feel lukewarm, like you've lost your passion for Jesus. This results in prayerlessness and feelings of hopelessness and apathy in worship. Can you see the connection? Once the coiling begins, it affects every organ in your body and it doesn't take long to snuff you out. Put in spiritual terms, when you feel the onset of a Python attack, you have to act quickly. You aren't likely to die, but it can set you back physically and spiritually for days or weeks or months if you don't resist it.

After a python snake cuts off your blood and oxygen, it swallows you. Python snakes can swallow their victims in an hour, denoting urgency is again key. The Python spirit wants to swallow your destiny. Consider one definition of swallow is "to take in so as to envelope; withdraw from sight; assimilate or absorb," according to *Dictionary.com*. Python will swallow like water—or pour out false water to engulf you in deception.

Noteworthy is Revelation 12:15-16: *"And the serpent poured water like a river out of his mouth after the woman, so that he might cause her to be swept away with the flood. But the earth helped the woman, and the earth opened its mouth and drank up the river which the dragon poured out of his mouth."* This demands further study in the context of water spirits as it is a strategy clearly exposed. The serpent aimed to destroy the woman with a deluge of water.

Although this has eschatological meaning, you can bring this down to its simplest terms. One of the serpent's tactics is to sweep the church away—and you are the Church—with a flood of deception. This water pouring out like a river could speak of corrupt doctrine. Indeed, one translation of the word "mouth" in Revelation 12:15 means "edge of a sword," according to *The KJV New Testament Greek Lexicon.*

Water is a literal translation. From the Greek word *hudor,* it speaks of water in rivers, in fountains, in pools. It points to the water of the deluge and water in any of the earth's repositories and of the waves of the sea. The serpent didn't release a mere trickle of water, but a stream, a river, a torrent, and a flood.

When Python attacks, it literally feels like a torrent, which is officially defined a "tumultuous outpouring: rush; a violent stream of a liquid (such as water or lava)," according to *Merriam-Webster.* Python will not lead you beside the still waters. Python rushes at you in violence with a demonic outpouring of witchcraft. Remember, this spirit is essentially a spirit of divination.

Was the Serpent in the Garden a Python?

Snakes and serpents are mentioned more than 80 times in the Bible. There is no difference between a snake and a serpent. One is a synonym for the other. Could it be possible that the serpent in the Garden of Eden was a python?

The serpent is symbolic of the fall of humankind. But make no mistake, satan actually used a real snake to tempt humankind. Despite our dominion over every creeping thing, humankind was deceived by that over which he had authority. That's something to reflect on in our battle against marine demons. God cursed the serpent above all animals (see Genesis 3:14).

Again, could it be possible the serpent in the Garden of Eden was a python? We know there was a river running out of Eden to water The Garden and shot off into four riverheads: Pishon, Gihon, Tigris, and Euphrates. Adam was charged with tending The Garden, and God allowed satan, in the form of a serpent, to enter into this place of paradise and talk to His people. The result: this serpent spewed lies at them. The serpent tempted them to sin, essentially squeezing God's life out them, introducing fear, guilt, and shame, and causing them to isolate themselves from God.

Noteworthy is the fact that when the Python spirit attacked Paul and Silas, it left them naked. When the serpent in The Garden attacked Adam and Eve, it also left them naked (see Genesis 3:10). The serpent brought a spiritual death to Adam and Eve—a separation from God, their Creator and Life-Giver. Had the mother and father of humankind not fallen to the serpent's lies, they would have lived forever by consuming fruit from the tree of life in the presence of God.

Was it a python in the Garden of Eden? A cobra? A boa constrictor? We don't know, but it is true the python is a type of serpent—and they are crafty. In fact, Genesis 3:1 says the serpent was *"more crafty than any beast of the field."* Other Bible translations say *"the shrewdest of all the wild animals the Lord God had made"* (New Living Translation), or *"most cunning"* (Holman), or *"more clever"* (International Standard Version), or *"more shrewd"* (New English Translation), or *"more subtle"* (King James Version), or *"more astute"* (Jubilee Bible 2000). If that's true, and it is, the Python spirit would fall under "most dangerous" marine demons category.

What did the serpent do? Led Eve into disobedience with a lie. Indeed, when you think of a snake, you think of sin. Jesus called serpents wise (see Matthew 10:16). The Bible speaks of the *"venom of serpents and the deadly poison of cobras"* (Deuteronomy 32:33) and the sharp tongues as a serpent (see Psalm 140:3). The Bible speaks of the serpent's bite and sting (Proverbs 23:32). The serpent's food is dust, which is representative of our flesh since humankind was made of dust (see Isaiah 65:25). Paul speaks of the destroying capacity of the serpent (see 1 Corinthians 10:9) and the deceptive capacity of the serpent (2 Corinthians 11:3).

Thank God, He has authority to tread and trample upon them (Luke 10:19). Psalm 91:13 assures us, *"You will tread upon the lion and the cobra, the young lion and the serpent you will trample down."*

Endnotes

1. Amy Gigi Alexander, "The last guardians of a python spirit," *BBC,* May 26, 2017; http://www.bbc.com/travel/story/20170519-the-last-guardians-of-a-python-spirit; accessed April 18, 2018.

2. https://www.britannica.com/topic/Apollo-Greek-mythology; accessed April 18, 2018.

3. Ker Than, "Strangulation of Sleeping Boys Puts Spotlight on Pythons, *National Geographic,* August 6, 2013; https://news.nationalgeographic.com/news/2013/08/130806-python-strangles-kids-canada-snakes/; accessed April 18, 2018.

4. Colin Fernandez, "Pythons kill by heart attack: Snakes actually cut off the blood supply of their prey rather than kill them by suffocation," *UK Daily Mail,* July 22, 2015; http://www.dailymail.co.uk/news/article-3171522/Pythons-kill-heart-attack-Snakes-actually-cut-blood-supply-prey-kill-suffocation.html; accessed April 18, 2018.

Chapter 5

PUTTING
PYTHON UNDER YOUR FEET

I N the wild, pythons are classified as opportunistic hunters that lay low until they are ready to strike their target. Pythons are also called opportunistic feeders or ambush predators. All of these terms describe the nature of this insidious spirit's attack. It's strategic, patient, yet aggressive.

Make no mistake, pythons are hunting. They will take any opportunity they can find to steal, kill, and destroy your prayer life—your hopes and dreams. They are predatory creatures that will set a carefully laid ambush, which *Merriam-Webster* defines as "a surprise attack from a hidden place." In other words, most of Python's victims never see it coming. It's slow moving, often sedentary as it observes the landscape, waiting for an unsuspecting victim to cross its path.

While wolves and other animals hunt in packs, pythons hunt alone. Pythons are not intimidated by prey that is larger or seemingly more powerful than they are. These coiling serpents have successfully attacked lions and elephants—even humans.

When pythons attack their prey in the wild, they strike from the side or the back, but when they are in defensive mode, they attack from the front.[1]

News story after news story gives accounts of pythons attacking humans from behind. This is telling. When the girl with the spirit of divination attacked Paul and Silas, the Bible says she followed them. This Python spirit came in from the rear; it was hunting the apostles from behind.

In the story of a farmer who was attacked by a python who swallowed him whole, *USA Today* reports, "Pythons bite first and would attack a human in two ways: 1. A startled snake could bite as a form of defense; 2. The python stealthily lies in wait along a game trail, edges of waterways or any other place where they would find unsuspecting prey.... Reticulated pythons bite first."[2]

Catch that. Some pythons bite first. Not all pythons—but some pythons. Part of Python's attack may be to bite you... to remind you of wounds from your past. It's easier to go in for the kill against a target that is wounded. One of Python's strategies, then, is to wound you by influencing someone— whether someone close to you or an absolute stranger—to you to "bite" you or to put pressure on hurts and wounds in your soul that are not healed. This tactic aims to effectively woo you out of spirit-minded status to soul-minded status so you won't discern its coiling.

In the natural, scientists say pythons don't attack humans unless they are provoked or stressed. The lesson: Don't poke a python. *The Washington Post* reports that Robert Nabadan was riding his moped home from work when he saw a giant python lying across the road. His mistake: he tried to move it. "The python latched onto his arm and began to coil...At some point, it also bit his head. He was able to dislodge the animal, possibly with a machete, but not before he was seriously injured."[3] Python saw the man as a threat and attacked.

However, pythons can, do, and have attacked unprovoked. Two boys—a four-year-old and a six-year-old, were strangled in their sleep when a python escaped its cage, worked through the air ducts, found its way into their apartment below, and killed the children.[4] And in Canada, a man—supposedly an experienced snake handler—was killed by his pet python, demonstrating the reality of a phrase I often use, "You can't play pattycake with the devil."[5]

The lesson here: python snakes can attack provoked or unprovoked—and so can Python spirits. You don't need to have an open door for Python to slither through. You don't have to be living in sin. Like Paul and Silas, you provoke a Python when you enter into certain regions where it has a stronghold and start doing the work of the ministry.

At the same, time, it's not wise to purposely provoke a Python spirit or any other spirit. You can provoke a Python spirit in pride by going on the offense against this serpent when it's not attacking you just to show your knowledge of warfare. You can also provoke a Python spirit by coming against it with wrong discernment when it is not coming against you. No matter how experienced you are in warfare, you need discernment and humility.

How a Snake Thinks and Moves

In order to defeat the Python spirit, it's helpful to understand how snakes think—and how we think about snakes. Humans are conditioned to fear snakes, even though some are absolutely harmless. Jesus told His apostles to be as wise as serpents (see Matthew 10:16). We have the wisdom of God, which makes us more wise than the enemy. Yet in the heat of battle we must understand how the enemy thinks—what is motivating him, how he is strategizing against us, etc.

The word "wise" in Matthew 10:16 comes from the Greek word *phronimos*. According to *The King James New Testament Greek Lexicon*, it means "intelligent, wise, prudent, i.e. mindful of one's interests." *Strong's* definition is "thoughtful, i.e. sagacious or discreet (implying a cautious character" and "practical skill or acumen" and "indicates rather intelligence or mental acquirement; in a bad sense conceited."

The devil is definitely conceited and always overplays his hand. The same is true of Python. Jesus wasn't telling us to be conceited like a snake, but to be intelligent in battle, wise in warfare, prudent in our approach, mindful of His interests, cautious in the fight, and to develop our skills in the skirmish. The enemy has spent thousands of years studying humankind. We're only here for 75 years, on average, and don't have nearly enough time—nor would we want to spend all our time—studying the devil. But, again, we must not be ignorant of his devices (see 2 Corinthians 2:11).

Rick Renner, an author and church planter who moved his family to the Soviet Union, has some good thoughts on how snakes think. He says, "When serpents move into a new territory, they don't make a lot of noise about it. They come in quietly and unannounced—in camouflaged." "Snakes," he explains, "evaluate new situations to see where they can hide from attack and where they can find easy kills. Most spiritual warriors I know come in with a loud bang and alert every devil in hell that they are in warfare mode when most of the demons were not targeting them. This is not wisdom!"[6]

"Serpents," Renner goes on, "are wise enough to know when to seize the moment and strike. They understand there's a kairos time to attack. The same is true in spiritual warfare, which is why we have to let God lead us in triumph in Christ Jesus (see 2 Corinthians 2:14). We need to submit to the Holy Spirit's leadership in the realm of spiritual warfare if we want radical effectiveness."

It's also helpful to consider how snakes move. Solomon wrote in Proverbs 30:18 that there are three things that were too wonderful to him and four he did not understand. One of them was *the way of a serpent on the rock.* The Hebrew word for "way" in Proverbs 30:19 is this context is "manner, habit, way."

Solomon was saying he didn't understand how the snake moved on a rock. *Pulpit Commentary* suggests this refers to how the serpent could move on the surface without leaving any track. *Gill's Exposition of the Entire Bible* speaks of how it "leaves no impression, no footsteps by which it can be traced." Sometimes, the Python's work in our lives is so subtle that we don't immediately discern its tracks—or stop it dead in its tracks—which is why we need to be wise like the serpent. Remember, the snake moves into a territory camouflaged.

Apparently, serpents used to have legs because when God cursed the snake, He said, *"Because you have done this, cursed are you more than all cattle, and more than every beast of the field; on your belly you will go, and dust you will eat all the days of your life"* (Genesis 3:14).

Although some commentators debate whether the serpent had legs, most agree it did. Not having legs slows the serpent down. They have to creep on their bellies using wavy, windy movements. That would seem to give us some advantage in the battle until they get close enough to strike. In other words, we have time to discern the approach of Python, but once Python moves close enough to bite or begins coiling around us the real battle rages.

Wanted: Python Killers

As I wrote in my book, *The Spiritual Warfare Battle Plan*, this python spirit is a major influence in Florida where we have more houses of prayer per capita than any other state. Python is so spiritually active in our state that it has manifested with an overrun of natural pythons in the Everglades. Experts point to as many as 100,000 Burmese pythons in the Florida Everglades that are reproducing rapidly. This snake is driving down populations of opossums, bobcats, and raccoons and even swallows deer and alligators whole.

Python killers are wage earners in Florida, where there is an overrun of these predators in the Florida Everglades. The South Florida Water Management District Governing Board is paying minimum wage to python hunters in order to protect the Everglades and eliminate invasive serpents from its public lands. The board reports:

> The invasive Burmese python, which breeds and multiplies quickly and has no natural predator in the Everglades ecosystem, has decimated native populations of wildlife. The more of these snakes that can be eliminated, especially females and their eggs, the better chance future generations of native

wildlife will have to thrive in the Everglades ecosystem that Floridians have invested billions of dollars to restore.

Twenty-five professional python hunters led the charge and killed 700 pythons in just a few months. The church needs "professional Python killers," those who know their authority over this spirit. But many in the church still don't understand how to survive a Python attack.

Naturally speaking, one way to survive a python attack is to pull out a knife. Spiritually speaking, you wield the Sword of the Spirit, which is the Word of God (see Ephesians 6:12). You can't just swing the Sword one time. You have to keep swinging it until you are free from the Python's coils. Naturally speaking, spraying a python with water can cause it to let go. We can use the water of the Word. We use praise and worship—and we shake off the attack. Here's the model in Scripture, found in Acts 16:25-28:

> *But about midnight Paul and Silas were praying and singing hymns of praise to God, and the prisoners were listening to them; and suddenly there came a great earthquake, so that the foundations of the prison house were shaken; and immediately all the doors were opened and everyone's chains were unfastened. When the jailer awoke and saw the prison doors opened, he drew his sword and was about to kill himself, supposing that the prisoners had escaped. But Paul cried out with a loud voice, saying, "Do not harm yourself, for we are all here!"*

At about midnight—when it looked like all hope was lost—the apostles were praying and praising. What's interesting is some commentators suggest this was a habitual practice that, despite the Python's bondage, Paul and Silas refused to abandon. *Ellicott's Commentary for English Readers* says, "The act was, we may believe, habitual, and they would not intermit it even in the dungeon, and fastened as they were, so that they could not kneel. The hymn may have been one of the prayer-psalms of David, or possibly one of those, of which Pliny speaks in his letters, and which may well have been in use half a century earlier, in which men offered adoration to Christ as God."

Therein lies a spiritual warfare tip against Python, which comes to squeeze out your prayer life. Pray anyway. Praise anyway. Python's pressure makes you want to do anything but pray or praise. Putting godly discipline to work to pray and praise even when it looks like nothing is changing cuts off the head of this snake. Paul and Silas may have been praying David-style "deliver me" prayers and singing about the goodness of God in the face of their enemies. Their prayer was effective. It caused the ground to shake. Paul and Silas literally shook off the attack.

Paul demonstrates another form of shaking off the serpent attack while he was stranded on the Island of Malta. Acts 28:3-5 tells us:

> *When Paul had gathered a bundle of sticks and laid them on the fire, a viper came out because of the heat and fastened itself on his hand. When the natives saw the creature hanging from his hand, they began saying to one another, "Undoubtedly this man is a murderer, and though he has been saved from the sea, justice has not allowed him to live." However he shook the creature off into the fire and suffered no harm.*

Travailing Prayer That Brings Deliverance

When it comes to spiritual warfare—and intercession—many times we don't know how to pray as we ought. We sense spiritual oppression trying to discourage us, demons harassing people we love, or principalities settling over our city like a dark rain cloud—but we don't always have revelation about the enemy we're fighting.

When that happens, I always do one thing: pray in the Spirit—and I don't stop praying in the Spirit until that oppression lifts or until I have a Spirit-inspired strategy to wrestle against what's wrestling against me. I wrestle from a place of victory, but I don't wrestle presumptuously. I need the Holy Spirit to show me how to pray—and sometimes that prayer includes travail. This is scriptural:

> *Likewise the Spirit also helps in our weaknesses. For we do not know what we should pray for as we ought, but the Spirit Himself makes intercession for us with groanings which cannot be uttered. Now He who searches the hearts knows what the mind of the Spirit is, because He makes intercession for the saints according to the will of God* (Romans 8:26-27 NKJV).

Notice that Paul wrote about *"groanings which cannot be uttered."* Here he's talking about one manifestation of travailing prayer. The Greek word for "groanings" in that Scripture is *stenagmos,* which simply means a groaning or a sigh.

Of course, the Holy Spirit is doing the groaning through us. We can't work up this type of prayer by our will. It's a spiritual response to a prayer burden. Travail has to be Spirit-led, or it's just soulish or fleshly. Nevertheless, travail is a genuine form of prayer that can break through when nothing else does. The Greek word "travail" is found several times in the New Testament (and many more times in the Old).

When Jesus talked about the pregnant woman who had sorrow in travail (see John 16:21), He was referring to *tikto,* which means "to bring forth, bear, produce (fruit from the seed); of a woman giving birth; of the earth bringing forth its fruits." But when Paul was talking about interceding for the Thessalonians (see 1 Thessalonians 2:9), the Greek word for travail is *mochthos,* which means a hard and difficult labor, toil, travail, hardship, distress.

Hebrew words for travail include *yalad,* which also brings in the connotation of helping: "to cause or help to bring forth; to assist or tend to as a midwife" (see Genesis 38:27); *"telaah,"* which implies seeking deliverance from toil, hardship, distress, weariness (see Exodus 18:8); *'inyan,* which refers to an occupation, task, job (see Ecclesiastes 1:13); *'amal,* which refers to toil, trouble, labor (see Isaiah 23:4); and *challah,* which means to be or become grieved, be or become sorry (see Isaiah 53:11).

Most of the time, travailing prayer is a birthing prayer—it births something you've been carrying in your heart that God wants to deliver. But it can also be a deliverance prayer. In this verse, travail is used in a deliverance context: *"And Moses told his father-in-law all that the Lord had done unto Pharaoh and to the Egyptians for Israel's sake, and all the travail that had come upon them by the way, and how the Lord delivered them"* (Exodus 18:8 KJV).

Sometimes, when the enemy gets an advantage on us (see 2 Corinthians 2:11), another person, or even a region, the Spirit of God will lead you into travailing prayer. You'll serve as a midwife and toil in prayer to help bring forth God's purposes—to birth His will in the earth—which may also mean deliverance from the kingdom of darkness.

Many times before travailing prayer comes upon you, you'll feel grieved, heavy, or otherwise burdened. Less experienced intercessors may believe they are under spiritual attack—and they may be—but it's often the Holy Spirit moving on your spirit to engage in travail with Him. Notice I say, "with Him." Again, you can't stir up travail in your soul or your flesh. It is Spirit-inspired. The important thing to know is that when you sense this coming on you, you need to yield to the Holy Spirit to birth His purposes.

Travail is not prayer led by emotions, though you may appear emotional as you enter travail with weeping and wailing and groaning like a woman birthing a child. Because of its intensity, some churches have relegated intercession to a back room in the church and essentially thrown the baby out with the breakthrough bathwater. But it's vital that we cooperate with the Holy Spirit when He wants to use us as a midwife to birth or deliver, even if you have to excuse yourself from the prayer meeting to avoid confusing those who are not familiar with this type of intercession.

Letting the Holy Spirit Pray Through You

With all this in mind, let's look at Romans 8 again:

> *For we know that the whole creation groans and labors with birth pangs together until now. Not only that, but we also who have the firstfruits of the Spirit, even we ourselves groan within ourselves, eagerly waiting for the adoption, the redemption of our body. For we were saved in this hope, but hope that is seen is not hope; for why does one still hope for what he sees? But if we hope for what we do not see, we eagerly wait for it with perseverance.*

> *Likewise the Spirit also helps in our weaknesses. For we do not know what we should pray for as we ought, but the Spirit Himself makes intercession for us with groanings which cannot be uttered. Now He who searches the hearts knows what the mind of the Spirit is, because He makes intercession for the saints according to the will of God* (Romans 8:22-27 NKJV).

The will of God is to birth His purposes. The will of God is to deliver people from the bonds of satan. The will of God is that we cooperate with His Holy Spirit, laboring in all manner of prayer to prevail in the wrestling match against principalities, powers, rulers of the darkness of this age, and spiritual hosts of wickedness in the heavenly places (see Ephesians 6:12). Sometimes all manner of prayer includes travail. Amen.

A Prayer Against Python's Pressure

Father, thank You for the blood of the Lamb and the power in the name of Jesus to crush the head of the snake—to put Python under my feet even when it's trying to coil around my mind and body to wreak havoc on my thoughts and bring physical manifestations of chocking in my body.

Thank You, Strong and Mighty Lord, for the delegated authority you've given me in Christ. In the mighty name of Jesus, the name above all names—the name above water spirits and marine demons—I take authority over every expression of Python's attack in my life. I break Python's power over my mind, will, and emotions. I break the Python's grip on my finances and my friendships. I break the power of Python's effect on my physical body. I command these symptoms to go, in Jesus' name.

I sever Python's coils from around me, working to constrict the flow of God's power in my life. I say *Dunamis* power trumps Python's power in my life and the anointing breaks the yoke of bondage Python has twisted around my neck. I annihilate Python's serpentine plans in every area of my life and declare I am free from this slithering assignment, in Jesus' name.

I praise You and You alone, Lord. I worship You and You alone. I thank You that where Your presence is, there is fullness of joy and the enemy of my soul must flee when I submit my heart to You, in Jesus' name.

Endnotes

1. Megan Gannon, "Florida's Python Invaders Rarely Attack People Unprovoked," *LiveScience,* March 12, 2014; https://www.livescience.com/44033-florida-pythons-rarely-attack-people.html; accessed April 19, 2018.

2. Sean Rossman, "Pythons can kill a human in minutes and swallow them in an hour," *USA TODAY,* March 30, 2017; https://www.usatoday.

com/story/news/nation-now/2017/03/30/pythons-can-kill-human-minutes-and-swallow-them-hour/99824246/; accessed April 19, 2018.

3. Cleve R. Wootson Jr., "Giant pythons keep attacking people in Indonesia—and humans might be to blame," *WashingtonPost.com World Views,* October 4, 2017; https://www.washingtonpost.com/news/worldviews/ wp/2017/10/04/giant-pythons-keep-attacking-indonesian-people-and-people-might-be-to-blame/?utm_term=.888815a6c6c6; accessed April 19, 2018.

4. Matt Smith and Jethro Mullen, "Snake kills two boys during sleepover, Canadian police say," *CNN,* August 7, 2013; http://www.cnn. com/2013/08/06/world/americas/canada-snake-deaths/index.html; accessed April 19, 2018.

5. Rozina Sabur, "Police investigate whether man was killed by python after his body was found alongside the pet snake," *UK The Telegraph,* September 25, 2017; http://www.telegraph.co.uk/news/2017/09/25/ police-investigate-whether-man-killed-python-body-found-alongside/; accessed April 19, 2018.

6. Rick Renner Ministries, "Learn to Think Like a Snake!"; September 7, 2016; http://www.renner.org/christian-living/learn-to-think-like-a-snake/; accessed April 19, 2018.

Chapter 6

LISTENING
TO LEVIATHAN'S LIES

J OB went through perhaps the worst-ever trial recorded in the Bible. Other than Christ being crucified on a cross, I don't read of any trial more excruciating on every level—family, finances, friendships, mind, and body—than what Job endured.

Let's take a closer look at Job. The Bible calls him a man who was *"blameless, upright, fearing God and turning away from evil"* (Job 1:1). He had seven sons and three daughters. He had 7,000 sheep, 3,000 camels, 500 yoke of oxen, 500 female donkeys, and many servants. In fact, the Bible classifies him as *"the greatest of all the men of the east"* (Job 1:3).

God allowed satan to test Job. I don't think satan himself completed the assignment. I believe he sent principalities and powers against the man of God to tag team against him.

Could it be possible Leviathan was one of those principalities? I believe so, as Job reveals more about this spirit than any other place in the Bible. Other Scriptures mention Leviathan, but God offers a discourse on this marine spirit in the pages of this painful book. Given the fervor of the attack against Job, I believe the Holy Spirit revealed the source for us to learn from.

What Is Leviathan?

The Bible mentions Leviathan in Job 3, 40, and 41, but that's not the only place this sea monster is found in Scripture. Isaiah points out Leviathan in Isaiah 27:1, noting the Lord will punish this *"fleeing serpent"* and *"kill the dragon who lives in the sea."* Psalm 74:14 speaks of God crushing the *"heads of Leviathan."* Psalm 104:26 points to Leviathan among the ships in the sea.

What is Leviathan and why is it so formidable? This spirit is mentioned in the Bible repeatedly and even made its way into the dictionary. *Merriam-Webster* defines Leviathan as "a sea monster defeated by Yahweh in various scriptural accounts; a large sea animal; the political state: a totalitarian state having a vast bureaucracy; something large or formidable."

According to *Eastman's Bible Dictionary*, leviathan is a transliterated Hebrew word *(livyathan)*, meaning "twisted," "coiled." The dictionary reveals: "In Job 3:8, Revised Version, and marg. of Authorized Version, it denotes the dragon which, according to Eastern tradition, is an enemy of light; in 41:1 the crocodile is meant; in Psalms 104:26 it 'denotes any large animal that moves by writhing or wriggling the body, the whale, the monsters of the deep.'"

Strong's Concordance defines Leviathan as "a wreathed animal or serpent, a large sea-monster. The constellation of the dragon, Draco; also as a symbol of Babylon: mourning." According to the *New World Encyclopedia,*[1] references to Leviathan in the Bible seem to have evolved from a confrontation between Baal and a seven-headed sea monster called Lotan, an Ugaritic orthography for the Hebrew Leviathan.

Some Bible commentators say Leviathan was the Nile crocodile, which carries the reputation of a vicious man-eater, according to *National Geographic.*[2] The crocodile is a patient, ambush predator that is known to lie in wait for weeks to catch its prey—and it's one of the largest reptiles in the world. Once they bite into flesh with their iron jaws, it's almost impossible to escape death. Nile crocodiles often hold their victims underwater to drown them.

God used Leviathan—a real rather than some mythological creature—in His discussion with Job to reveal to us how this spirit operates. It has more than one head. It twists words. It brings mourning. It's patient, waiting for an opportunity strike. It tries to drown its victims.

The Depth of Leviathan's Attack

As I said at the outset of this chapter, Job went through one of the worst trials recorded in the Bible. He had seven sons and three daughters. He had 7,000 sheep, 3,000 camels, 500 yoke of oxen, 500 female donkeys, and many servants. Spirits, predominantly led by Leviathan, attacked him in every area—and the first wave came as a demonic suddenly. Job 1:13-19 says:

> *Now on the day when his sons and his daughters were eating and drinking wine in their oldest brother's house, a messenger came to Job and said, "The oxen were plowing and the donkeys feeding beside them, and the Sabeans attacked and took them. They also slew the servants with the edge of the sword, and I alone have escaped to tell you."*
>
> *While he was still speaking, another also came and said, "The fire of God fell from heaven and burned up the sheep and the servants and consumed them, and I alone have escaped to tell you." While he was still speaking, another also came and said, "The Chaldeans formed three bands and made a raid on the camels and took them and slew the servants with the edge of the sword, and I alone have escaped to tell you."*
>
> *While he was still speaking, another also came and said, "Your sons and your daughters were eating and drinking wine in their oldest brother's house, and behold, a great wind came from across the wilderness and struck the four corners of the*

house, and it fell on the young people and they died, and I alone have escaped to tell you."

Since Job's reaction to all this trauma was to worship the Lord, satan went to God again asking for permission to attack his body—to press him past his natural limits with excruciating physical pain. It's important to note that many times in a demonic attack, the last area the enemy will target is the body. Job 2:7-8 tells us, *"Then Satan went out from the presence of the Lord and smote Job with sore boils from the sole of his foot to the crown of his head. And he took a potsherd to scrape himself while he was sitting among the ashes."*

In the midst of demonic attack, Job's friends offered him anything but comfort. Eliphaz came to tell him it was his fault because he had some hidden sin in his life (see Job 4:7-8). Bildad calls confirmed Eliphaz's poor prophecies (see Job 8:20). Finally, Zophar acted as a third witness to condemn Job in his battle (see Job 11:14-17). Even Job's wife told him to curse God and die (see Job 2:9). Job's heart attitude: *"Though He slay me, yet I will trust Him"* (Job 13:15 KJV).

What the Lord Revealed About Leviathan

The Lord went on a diatribe about Leviathan in Job 41. One has to ask: Why would the Lord spend so much time talking about Leviathan if it had nothing to do with the fierce attack on Job's life? Job was not a seaman. Rather, he owned cattle and oxen. Yet he was obviously familiar with Leviathan or the Lord would not have used it as an example to Job. God drew parallels Job would understand—and that He wants us to understand.

Let's look at the entirety of Job 41. Notice how the Lord in this chapter asks question after question after question. God is not asking Job because He doesn't know the answer. God wants Job to reflect on these things and receive revelation so he can defeat this foe.

"Can you draw out Leviathan with a fishhook? Or press down his tongue with a cord? Can you put a rope in his nose or pierce his jaw with a hook? Will he make many supplications to you, or will he speak to you soft words?" (Job 41:1-3).

People under the influence of a Leviathan spirit speak no soft words—they are harsh. They do not make supplication—that is, humble requests, but instead make demands. In our own power, we are no match for Leviathan spirits. When it comes to Leviathan, the battle is the Lord's.

"Will he make a covenant with you? Will you take him for a servant forever?" (Job 41:4). People under the influence of a Leviathan spirit will break covenants. They are too proud to serve.

"Will you play with him as with a bird, or will you bind him for your maidens? Will the traders bargain over him? Will they divide him among the merchants? Can you fill his skin with harpoons, or his head with fishing spears?" (Job 41:5-7) These verses indicate Leviathan is not a spirit to play with, but it also indicates part of this principality's nature—to mock.

The Hebrew word for "play" in this verse is *shachaq*. According to *The KJV Old Testament Hebrew Lexicon,* it means "to laugh, play, mock; to make sport, to jest, to laugh mockingly." Leviathan mocks its targets. *Merriam-Webster* defines mock as "to treat with contempt or ridicule: deride; to disappoint the hopes of; to defy, challenge; to imitate (something or someone closely): mimic." People under the influence of this spirit treat people with contempt. They walk in defiance. They challenge authority. Leviathan wants to disappoint your hopes and kill your dreams.

Lay your hand on him; remember the battle; you will not do it again! Behold, your expectation is false; will you be laid low even at the sight of him? No one is so fierce that he dares to arouse him; who then is he that can stand before Me? Who has

> *given to Me that I should repay him? Whatever is under the whole heaven is Mine* (Job 41:8-11).

This is the third warning in this passage about coming directly against Leviathan. Leviathan is not a spirit to stir up. In other words, some weekend warriors tend to start calling out spirits and binding them with bravado. As a principality, Leviathan cannot be bound in the same way you would bind a spirit of fear. It's entrenched in regions and works on the minds of people rather than occupying a place in their souls as rejection or lust might. In these next verses, the Lord gets granular about Leviathan's characteristics.

Deceitful Reasoning

"I will not keep silence concerning his limbs, or his mighty strength, or his orderly frame" (Job 41:12). Mighty strength offers the concept of not only strength and might but also valor and bravery. It's translated elsewhere in the Bible as courage, mighty acts, mighty deeds, power, and triumph. Despite its terrifying appearance, the Lord describes Leviathan's "orderly frame," which actually translates as beauty and grace in *The NAS Old Testament Hebrew Lexicon*. Leviathan's reasoning can seem beautiful in the mind of the one it deceives. Leviathan's lies make its victim feel strong and courageous against opponents, which is a manifestation of pride.

Difficult to Contend With

"Who can strip off his outer armor? Who can come within his double mail?" (Job 41:13). Studying the Hebrew, the idea with "strip off" is especially telling in terms of how difficult it is to contend with Leviathan. Strip off comes from the Hebrew word *galah,* which means "carried away into exile, banished, betray, captives, deported, exposed, removed, revealed, and stripped," according to *The NAS Old Testament Hebrew Lexicon.*

The point is, who can banish Leviathan? Leviathan and other demons will be roaming the earth and sea until Jesus returns to bring ultimate victory. Pride won't defeat pride. Put another way, haughty spiritual warriors will not exile this haughty spirit.

Flapping Jaws Speaking Proud Imaginations

What is Leviathan's *"double mail"*? The lexicon defines this as "jaw." The idea here is "who can close his mouth?" You can cast down Leviathan's imaginations, but ultimately this spirit is not going to stop whispering to humankind until the Lord returns. You can rise above it in your personal battle, but that doesn't stop Leviathan from flapping his jaws to those around you—or flapping his jaws at you.

A Spiritual Terrorist

"Who can open the doors of his face? Around his teeth there is terror" (Job 41:14). The Leviathan spirit will bring terror and dread into your life. Terror is beyond fear—it's a state of intense fear, according to *Merriam-Webster*. It causes anxiety. Leviathan is a spiritual terrorist, bringing what our dictionary calls "violent and destructive acts (such as bombing) committed by groups in order to intimidate a population or government into granting their demands." Leviathan essentially launched a series of terror attacks against Job—his family, his livestock, his body, and his relationships.

Impenetrable Pride

"His strong scales are his pride, shut up as with a tight seal. One is so near to another that no air can come between them. They are joined one to another; they clasp each other and cannot be separated" (Job 41:15-17). His strong scales are his pride! What a picture! The Hebrew word for scales in this verse is *magen,* which means a shield or buckler, according to *The NAS Old Testament*

Hebrew Lexicon. The notion here is that Leviathan's pride is impenetrable. You can't break through it. When someone is under the influence of this marine demon, it's as if scales are over their eyes and they see through the lens of pride. There is no reasoning with them.

Sudden, Blinding Attacks

"His sneezes flash forth light, and his eyes are like the eyelids of the morning" (Job 41:18). This is a telling verse. Think about sneezing. According to *Merriam-Webster*, it means "to make a sudden violent spasmodic audible expiration of breath...." The Hebrew word "flash" actually means "boastful" in our lexicon. Leviathan makes sudden, violent, spasmodic boastful moves against his victims. The light he flashes blinds his victims with pride.

Words That Burn and Vision-Clouding Smoke

"Out of his mouth go burning torches; sparks of fire leap forth. Out of his nostrils smoke goes forth as from a boiling pot and burning rushes. His breath kindles coals, and a flame goes forth from his mouth" (Job 41:19-21). Leviathan's words will burn you and his smoke will cloud your vision and bring confusion.

Stiff-Necked and Stubborn

"In his neck lodges strength, and dismay leaps before him. The folds of his flesh are joined together, firm on him and immovable. His heart is as hard as a stone, even as hard as a lower millstone" (Job 41:22-24). Here again we see the concept of pride. People under Leviathan's influence are stiff-necked. *The International Standard Bible Encyclopedia* tells us: "As it is figuratively used, both in the Old Testament and in the New Testament, the word means 'stubborn,' 'untractable,' 'not to be led.'" That's haughty.

In Acts 7:51, Stephen was speaking to the religious Pharisees of his day. He described them as stiff-necked and resisting the Holy Spirit. God resists the proud, but gives grace to the humble (see James 4:6). The proud Pharaoh of Egypt in Moses' day was stiff-necked and hard-hearted. I don't think it's any coincidence that he lived near the Nile river, which was full of crocodiles. A Leviathan spirit was demonstrating its strength in the region.

Releasing Fear and Crushing Bewilderment

"When he raises himself up, the mighty fear; because of the crashing they are bewildered" (Job 41:25). When Leviathan raises itself up against you in its wrath, it will bring an assignment of fear with it. Leviathan wants to exalt itself in your life with injections of prideful reasoning that puffs up your heart. What about the crashing? Crashing in this verse comes from the Hebrew word *sheber,* which means breaking, fracturing, crushing, breaching, crashing, ruining, and shattering, according to *The NASB Old Testament Greek Lexicon.*

Leviathan works to crush its target's hopes and dreams, breaking up relationships, inspiring covenantal breaches, ruining business deals, shattering financial security, fracturing mindsets, and the like—through pride. Job 41:25 says because of the crashing they are bewildered. Bewildered in this verse comes from the Hebrew word *chata.* It means to sin, miss, go wrong, incur guilt, forfeit, or bear loss, according to the lexicon. Leviathan's influence or attack can tempt you to engage in the sin of pride or some other sin as you fight against an unseen enemy working through the people around you or in the territory in which you live.

Fierce in Battle

"The sword that reaches him cannot avail, nor the spear, the dart or the javelin. He regards iron as straw, bronze as rotten wood. The arrow cannot make him flee; slingstones are turned into stubble for him. Clubs are regarded as stubble; he laughs at the rattling of the javelin" (Job 41:26-29). Again, this demonstrates

how fierce Leviathan is—and how difficult to defeat. Your typical spiritual warfare rituals are likely to fall to the ground in Leviathan's face.

Fragrance of Death

"His underparts are like sharp potsherds; he spreads out like a threshing sledge on the mire. He makes the depths boil like a pot; he makes the sea like a jar of ointment" (Job 41:30-31). The repeated metaphor in these verses is sharp, spreading, spreading and seething. Use of the word ointment is telling. Ointments can be cosmetic, for burial, medicinal, or used in rituals, according to *Smith's Bible Dictionary*. I believe Leviathan has an ointment, or a fragrance, of death. Some Christians can "smell" in the spirit, which is a manifestation of discernment.

Leaves a Visible Trail

"Behind him he makes a wake to shine; One would think the deep to be gray-haired. Nothing on earth is like him, one made without fear. He looks on everything that is high; he is king over all the sons of pride" (Job 41:32-34). The Hebrew word "wake" in this verse is *nathiyb*. According to our lexicon, it means "troden with the feet, path, pathway." So the Lord is saying he leaves a visible trail. You know a spirit has wreaked havoc, even if you don't know what spirit it was. The Lord's conclusion of the Leviathan discourse reiterates the fierceness of this marine demon and the root of pride that drives it.

Endnotes

1. *New World Encyclopedia,* "Leviathan"; http://www.newworldencyclopedia.org/entry/Leviathan; accessed April 19, 2018.

2. *National Geographic,* "Nile Crocodile"; https://www.nationalgeographic.com/animals/reptiles/n/nile-crocodile/; accessed April 19, 2018.

Chapter 7

LOOSING

LEVIATHAN'S HOLD ON YOUR LIFE

CROCODILE attacks are on the rise. A headline in *The Guardian* from 2017 reads, "Out of control: saltwater crocodile attacks terrorize Solomon Islands."[1] Remember, the Leviathan spirit is compared to a crocodile and operates in terror and dread. The Solomon Islands have set up a special police crocodile control unit to deal with the growing number of attacks.

"Crocodile attacks began to increase in the years after Ramsi arrived, and we believe it is because the villagers didn't have guns any more to protect themselves and shoot the crocodiles," Superintendent Stanley Riolo told *The Guardian*. "We are currently in discussions to plan a post-Ramsi crocodile control programme, but at the moment our only option is shooting them. There have been so many attacks: the crocodile population is out of control."

And it's not just the islands east of Papua New Guinea that are witnessing this terror. *The International Business Times* reports, "In northern Australia, you are never more than a couple of hours away from being eaten by a saltwater crocodile."[2]

Zimbabwe, too, is reporting a rise in crocodile attacks after heavy rains and flooded rivers.[3] Malaysia is also seeing the surge. Malaysia's *Express* offers this headline: "Island besieged by deadly croc attacks mourns latest death after woman dragged into river."[4] For all the media reports of deaths associated with crocodile attacks, there are many more that go unreported.

As I've said before, if the natural parallels the spirit world—and I believe it does in many instances—this rise is telling. It speaks to the boastful, haughty rise of this marine demon named Leviathan in the last days. So how exactly does a crocodile attack and what can we learn from this as applied to Leviathan?

How Leviathan Attacks

We explored briefly some ways Leviathan attacks, blinding its victims with pride, terror, anxiety and the like, by exploring its distinct characteristics in the marine demon world. But looking at the predator aspect of this spirit is telling. Few survive a crocodile attack in the natural realm. Consider this account of a real-life crocodile attack from *The Australian:*

> Speaking from grim experience, Bairstow, 34, says crocs strike in a blur of horror, without warning. The first he knew of the one that went for him was when it burst out of Trunding Creek about 3.30pm on a steamy Wednesday, after he had knocked off work in Weipa to go fishing. The crocodile latched on to his left leg and dragged him down the muddy creek bank. There was no pain as it bit down; all he could do was grab at the base of a mangrove tree while he was pulled into the water. Bairstow can't remember whether he was yelling. A surreal and numbing form of confusion descended, something other survivors have spoken of.

Bairstow's only conscious thought was to hang on. The crocodile was growling, low and menacing, and he was looking into its eyes while it tugged at his legs. Then, with a mighty flick of its thorny tail, it popped his knees "like matchsticks," rolling over and over to break his grip on the mangrove stem. For a moment it released him, only to bite down again and explode into another death roll. In desperation, he thrust his left hand into the croc's mouth. The index finger was so badly gashed it later had to be amputated. Bairstow gouged at the brute's eyes; he could smell its putrid breath from his position half in, half out of the water. The minutes crawled by like hours.

Suddenly, he felt something give. Had the crocodile tired? Bairstow thought he could feel himself clawing his way up the muddy bank but when he looked down the jaws were still clamped around his legs and "I realised it was just the skin stretching."

His arms were shaking. They had no strength left in them. This was it, then. He let go of the mangrove, let go of life. The crocodile dragged him into the creek. "I took a breath and went under the water not expecting to come up," he remembers. But the strangest thing happened. The thrashing crocodile was unable to do anything more to him. "The water was only two feet (60cm) deep, not enough for it to drown me." Bairstow yelled and yelled because making a racket was all he could do.[5]

Ultimately, Bairstow was rescued. You can battle off a Leviathan attack, but you need to discern the attack. Because the crocodile's eyes, nose, and ears are high up on top of its skull, *National Geographic* reports it can still hear, see, and breathe when it's almost completely under water—and a protective membrane closes over its eyes, serving as swimming goggles.[6] That makes it especially difficult to detect. Meanwhile, crocodiles have a strong sense of smell—which equates to discernment in the spiritual realm.

Crocodiles aren't likely to chase you down and overtake you. They use a surprise attack, lunging out of seemingly nowhere. Crocodiles often hunt together, rather than swimming solo. *National Geographic* reports the males are territorial, defending a length of shoreline. Noteworthy is the fact that, "The muscles that close a crocodile's jaws are capable of generating enormous power, yet the muscles that open the jaws have little strength. Even a rubber band around the snout of a crocodile is sufficient to prevent it from opening its mouth."[7]

These details are more than telling—they are chilling. Leviathan is not hunting you, not really. You could be on its radar screen but this spirit is likely to wait for you to get close enough to it to strike rather than seeking you out. I believe the more we move in pride, the closer we align ourselves with Leviathan and the more likely we are to come under its influence.

Crocodile attacks are often seasonal. This is fascinating as we know the enemy always comes at an opportune time. There's a *kairos* time for a Leviathan attack against your life.

When is a strategic season for Leviathan attack? Crocodiles are most likely to attack in seasons of rain, temperature increases, and breeding season. Translating this to the natural, rain demonstrates God's blessing or the Holy Spirit falling—or on the contrary storms. During times of promotion or moves of God in your life, watch out for Leviathan. But watch for him when all hell seems to be raging against you already.

Crocodiles attack during temperature increases. When you get on fire for God, watch out for Leviathan—remember it's His fire stirring in you. During breeding season crocodiles attack. Beware of Leviathan in seasons of spiritual growth or spiritual birthing. All of these times are prime times for pride in your heart to open the door to Leviathan.

Was Job Walking in Spiritual Pride?

Some Bible commentators suggest the Lord was showing Job he had spiritual pride through his discussion of Leviathan in Job 41. Pride can open the door to spiritual attack—and spiritual pride is the worst kind of pride. Spiritual pride is what got lucifer evicted from heaven. Still, others claim fear was the open door to Job's life. He made sacrifices to the Lord on behalf of his children every day just in case they sinned (see Job 1:5).

So, who is right? Or are both views right? Are pride and fear somehow connected? I had never thought of the possibility until studying this out. I started by looking up the definitions. Proud means "having or displaying excessive self-esteem," according to *Merriam-Webster*, and fear is "an unpleasant often strong emotion caused by anticipation or awareness of danger."

I didn't see an immediate connection, but I kept praying and studying. Usually, the proud seem to fear nothing—but the problem is the proud lack a fear of the Lord. God resists the proud and gives grace to the humble (see James 4:6). Pride is faith in one's self or one's righteousness or one's deeds rather than faith in God. Pride is the opposite of humility. Pride trusts itself more than it trusts God.

Job defended himself to his friends repeatedly. Was this pride? Defending yourself against false accusations isn't necessarily pride but it can be. Clearly, the Lord's diatribe on Leviathan aimed to show him a measure of self-righteousness he was walking in. Job 29:7-17 demonstrates this in the context of Job speaking of his righteous acts:

> *When I went out to the gate of the city, when I took my seat in the square, the young men saw me and hid themselves, and the old men arose and stood. The princes stopped talking and put their hands on their mouths; the voice of the nobles was hushed, and their tongue stuck to their palate. For when the ear heard, it called me blessed, and when the eye saw, it gave*

witness of me, because I delivered the poor who cried for help, and the orphan who had no helper.

The blessing of the one ready to perish came upon me, and I made the widow's heart sing for joy. I put on righteousness, and it clothed me; my justice was like a robe and a turban. I was eyes to the blind and feet to the lame. I was a father to the needy, and I investigated the case which I did not know. I broke the jaws of the wicked and snatched the prey from his teeth.

Leviathan Walks Through the Door of Spiritual Pride

The first and worst cause of error that prevails in our day is spiritual pride. So said Jonathan Edwards, a preacher, theologian, and missionary to Native Americans who lived in the 1700s.

Edwards went on to say that spiritual pride is the main door by which the devil comes into the hearts of those who are zealous for the advancement of Christ—the chief inlet of smoke from the bottomless pit to darken the mind and mislead the judgment, and the main handle by which satan takes hold of Christians to hinder a work of God. Powerful words!

If that was true in Edwards' day—and it was—then how much more is it true in our day? Some spiritual warriors take on Leviathan like it's a garden variety demon and find it destroys their relationships. Some church leaders take pride in their position or popularity and open the door to a downfall at Leviathan's hand.

Someone who is under Leviathan's influence sees him or herself as more discerning, more anointed, more eloquent, more revelatory, more important and, otherwise, well, more spiritual than you. Some of the ways spiritual pride manifests include self-righteousness, hypercritical attitudes, hypocrisy, scorning correction or guidance, putting on pretenses, and false humility.

Of course, God hates pride in any form, but I believe spiritual pride is the worst manifestation. It's so deceptive that the ones who walk in spiritual pride are too proud to consider that they may be suffering from this deplorable disease. In fact, spiritual pride mistakes the favor of people for the favor of God.

Jonah walked in a measure of self-righteousness and spiritual pride, as well as rebellion and stubbornness. The Lord told Jonah to go to Nineveh and preach against the wickedness of its society. Jonah's immediate response was to run away from the Lord and board a ship that was headed in the opposite direction toward Tarshish.

Jonah rebelled against the word of the Lord because he wanted Nineveh to experience the wrath of God instead of the mercy of God. Jonah knew that Jehovah would forgive the people there if his message brought them to repentance. That's a self-righteous stance. He no more deserved mercy than the inhabitants of Nineveh.

Jonah 1:17 tell us, *"The Lord appointed a great fish to swallow Jonah, and Johan was in the stomach of the fish for three days and three nights."* Some translations, including the International Standard Version, use the phrase *"large sea creature."* Children's Bible stories say it was a whale—and some Bible commentators say Leviathan was a whale. Did Jonah open himself up to a Leviathan attack through his self-righteous pride and rebellion?

Breaking Free from Leviathan

Whether Job and Jonah fell prey to Leviathan through pride could be debated until Jesus comes back. But the two men of God had similar experiences and they broke free with similar strategies. Given there is a clear connection between pride and Leviathan—and especially spiritual pride—we'll explore just how Job and Jonah escaped their trials.

Edwards concluded that until the disease of spiritual pride is cured, medicines are applied in vain to heal all other diseases. The good news is spiritual pride can be cured. The prescription is strong dose of conviction, repentance and humility—and I might say an ongoing effort to cooperate with the grace of God to walk in the fear of the Lord.

Job's endless defense against his friends' accusations did not free him. It was his humility. We find the account in Job 42, which, by the way, follows the Lord's intense description of Leviathan's pride in Job 41. Coincidence? Hardly. Job was loosed from Leviathan's grip when he stopped defending himself, saw the error of his ways through the grace of God's revelation in Job 41, and prayed for his friends. It takes humility to pray for those who have persecuted you in your time of trial. Job 42:10-17 offers the end of Job's story:

> *The Lord restored the fortunes of Job when he prayed for his friends, and the Lord increased all that Job had twofold. Then all his brothers and all his sisters and all who had known him before came to him, and they ate bread with him in his house; and they consoled him and comforted him for all the adversities that the Lord had brought on him. And each one gave him one piece of money, and each a ring of gold.*
>
> *The Lord blessed the latter days of Job more than his beginning; and he had 14,000 sheep and 6,000 camels and 1,000 yoke of oxen and 1,000 female donkeys. He had seven sons and three daughters. He named the first Jemimah, and the second Keziah, and the third Keren-happuch. In all the land no women were found so fair as Job's daughters; and their father gave them inheritance among their brothers. After this, Job lived 140 years, and saw his sons and his grandsons, four generations. And Job died, an old man and full of days.*

Likewise, Jonah's display of humility through prayer is what delivered him from the great sea creature. Jonah 2 reveals:

> *Then Jonah prayed to the Lord his God from the stomach of the fish, and he said, "I called out of my distress to the Lord, and He answered me. I cried for help from the depth of Sheol; You heard my voice. For You had cast me into the deep, into the heart of the seas, and the current engulfed me. All Your breakers and billows passed over me. So I said, 'I have been expelled from Your sight. Nevertheless I will look again toward Your holy temple.'*
>
> *"Water encompassed me to the point of death. The great deep engulfed me, weeds were wrapped around my head. I descended to the roots of the mountains. The earth with its bars was around me forever, but You have brought up my life from the pit, O Lord my God. While I was fainting away, I remembered the Lord, and my prayer came to You, into Your holy temple. Those who regard vain idols forsake their faithfulness, but I will sacrifice to You with the voice of thanksgiving. That which I have vowed I will pay. Salvation is from the Lord." Then the Lord commanded the fish, and it vomited Jonah up onto the dry land.*

This is a battle the Lord fights for you when you take the posture of humility. Leviathan in Isaiah 27:1, noting the Lord will punish this *"fleeing serpent"* and *"kill the dragon who lives in the sea."* Psalm 74:14 speaks of God crushing the "heads of Leviathan."

We can't battle Leviathan in the flesh, yet the temptation is to rely on the flesh in warfare in subtle ways. We can take pride in our spiritual warfare skills—but pride in any area of our life can hinder our effectiveness in destroying strongholds. It's pride in any area of our life.

Of course, we all have a measure of pride in our carnal nature. But when the Holy Spirit is dealing with us about pride in some area—or when we see our own pride and don't cry out for the grace of humility—we're walking in sheer disobedience. The Bible says we are to have a *"readiness to revenge all disobedience, when your obedience is fulfilled"* (2 Corinthians 10:6 KJV).

I believe the more we seek to walk in obedience to the Word of God, the more effective we'll be in spiritual warfare. So we return once again to the admonition of James:

> *He gives more grace. Therefore He says: "God resists the proud, but gives grace to the humble." Therefore submit to God. Resist the devil and he will flee from you. Draw near to God and He will draw near to you. Cleanse your hands, you sinners; and purify your hearts, you double-minded* (James 4:6-8 NKJV).

In our flesh, we're no match for Leviathan or any other spirit. We need the power of the Holy Spirit to back up our authority in Christ to root out, pull down, destroy, throw down, build, and plant. We can't drive demons into obedience to the Word of God when we're blatantly disobeying the Word of God in any area, whether it's walking in pride or some other sin.

A Prayer to Loose You From Leviathan's Lies

Father, I come to You in the name of Jesus, asking for forgiveness and protection. I repent for any and every manifestation of haughtiness, pride, stubbornness, stiff-necked postures, and the like. Forgive me for allowing any corrupt communication to come out of my mouth.

I break any and all agreement with Leviathan's twisted influence against my mind and heart. Forgive me, Lord, in Jesus' name for entertaining Leviathan's thoughts and allowing myself to fall prey to this marine demon's hard-hearted agenda, in Jesus' name.

Father, help me to crucify my flesh so that my carnal nature does not rise up and lead me. Help me to be led by Your Spirit and Your Spirit alone so that I don't fall into Leviathan's trap, judging, criticizing, complaining—and fleeing when things get difficult. Help me to shut the voice of pride out of my life once and for all, resisting it at its onset. Help me to take every thought captive with the Word of God, in Jesus' name.

Now, I take authority over Leviathan's witchcraft in my life released through the haughty stance of others. I break the powers of Leviathan's fruit in my life, from sickness and disease to confusion and exhaustion. I stand against the forces of hell Leviathan has released into my life through the spiritual atmosphere in my city or cities I've traveled to. Help me to stand and withstand against sudden Leviathan attacks, in Jesus' name.

Endnotes

1. Eleanor Ainge Roy, "Out of Control": saltwater crocodile attacks terrorise Solomon Islands, *The Guardian,* July 24, 2017; https://www.theguardian.com/environment/2017/jul/25/saltwater-crocodile-attacks-solomon-islands; accessed April 19, 2018.

2. Adam Britton, "Increase in crocodile attacks? People living near predators will always be at some risk," *International Business Times,* March 24, 2017; http://www.ibtimes.co.uk/increase-crocodile-attacks-people-living-near-predators-will-always-be-some-risk-1613348; accessed April 19, 2018.

3. "Zimbabwe Rains See Rise in Croc Attacks," http://ewn.co.za/2017/04/18/zimbabwe-rains-see-rise-in-croc-attacks; accessed April 19, 2018.

4. Jon Austin, "Island besieged by deadly croc attacks mourns latest death after woman dragged into river," *UK Express,* June 5, 2015; https://www.express.co.uk/news/nature/582285/Island-deadly-crocodile-attacks-death-woman-dragged-river-saltwater-Borneo-Grace-Jamar; accessed April 19, 2018.

5. http://www.theaustralian.com.au/news/inquirer/facing-the-jaws-of-death-few-survive-a-crocodile-attack/news-story/605a6c88e5837d-81530dc203dd96a9af; accessed May 22, 2018.

6. *National Geographic,* "Crocodile Facts," February 10, 2012; http://channel.nationalgeographic.com/wild/built-for-the-kill/articles/crocodile-facts/; accessed April 19, 2018.

7. Ibid.

Chapter 8

DISCERNING
THE SNEAKY SQUID SPIRIT

WHEN my friend told me she saw a vision of herself with a big squid lodged atop her head, I knew enough about the unseen world to understand a spiritual attack was underway. What I didn't know was that a Sneaky Squid Spirit would soon start stalking me.

Right about now, you might be scratching your head and asking, with all sincerity—*What in the world is a Squid Spirit?* Essentially, it's a spirit of mind control but its affects go way beyond what you would think.

In his classic book *Demon Hit List,*[1] John Eckhardt lists mind control and defines it this way: "Octopus and squid spirits having tentacles; confusion, mental pressure, mental pain, migraine." Sounds a lot like witchcraft. I imagine it is a form of witchcraft. As I have taught for many years, there are many expressions—and many manifestations—of witchcraft.

In Eckhardt's *Deliverance and Spiritual Warfare Manual,*[2] he offers a deeper explanation of mind control: "Spirits that control the mind and affect the way a person thinks. If evil spirits can control the thoughts, they can defeat the individual (Proverbs 23:7). Mind control is a very important spirit in satan's arsenal."

A Natural Examination
With Spiritual Implications

In the natural, a squid is a cephalopod with eight short arms and two longer tentacles. Different than an octopus with its big round head, a squid has a long skinny body with fins on both sides.

Like an octopus, the squid has tentacles.

Merriam-Webster defines tentacles this way: "any of various elongate flexible usually tactile or prehensile processes borne by animals and especially invertebrates chiefly on the head or about the mouth." Tentacles are essentially what science calls a muscular hydrostat, which works sort of like a tongue. Muscular hydrostats manipulate—catch that word—things around it. People manipulate your mind with their tongues. Squids manipulate your mind with their sucker-laced tentacles.

To be sure, tentacles have lots of "suckers." The squid's suckers are even more effective than the octopus' in capturing prey. Squids were created almost like a combustion chamber with a piston that fires when something tries to escape the suckers. Remember Chinese finger traps from your childhood? Some call them Chinese handcuffs because once they are wrapped around your fingers it's hard to break free and the harder you try, the tighter the cuffs cling to your fingers.

Here's a lesson: We're not wrestling against flesh and blood (see Ephesians 6:12). We can't overcome a Squid attack in our flesh. The more we struggle in our flesh, the greater the hold this spirit seems to get on us. The more we get in our heads trying to figure things out, the more ground the Squid takes because the Squid is attacking our head (our mind).

Squids also have a chameleon persona. Reference.com reveals, "Squid have the largest nervous system in the animal kingdom. They have the ability to change colors because they have translucent skin. The colors come from chromatophores, which are pigment cells that are on the outside of the skin that expand or contract to show colors."

Spiritually speaking, this chameleon-like characteristic means it can change its behavior or appearance to stay hidden. It's sneaky! Squids are fast swimmers and some of them can even fly. Again, that's why you need discernment in any spiritual battle. Internet checklists and articles can be helpful if the Holy Spirit illuminates the truths within them, but we must ultimately wage prophetic warfare if we are going to win the battle.

Squids and octopuses are seen as elusive sea creatures that often defend themselves by releasing black ink that makes the water dark and cloudy so oceanic enemies can't see them. You might liken this to the enemy's smoke screen. A smoke screen is a military term that refers to a cloud of smoke that masks or cloaks military operations but is also used as a term to disguise or hide someone's true intentions.

When you begin to war against a Squid Spirit, you can expect an attack that works to further darken your discernment and cloud your mind with confusion. Squid ink is made up of mucus and a pigment called melanin. So when the squid attacks, it's like the enemy spitting in your face. Octopuses are a bit different. They can release poisoning venom that can make victims weak, paralyze, or even kill them. Octopuses also have a harder beak, which is used as a weapon in warfare.

The Squid's Pressuring Pain

Before we deal with the realm of mind control, let's look at the physical realm. Remember, the squid spirit manifests in our minds and bodies as confusion, mental pressure, mental pain, and migraines. Eckhardt writes, "Migraine headaches are caused by mind control spirits."[2] Although we think we know what these things mean, getting proper definitions helps us pinpoint the manifestations.

Confuse means "to disturb in mind or purpose: throw off," according to *Merriam-Webster*. We know God is not a God of confusion, but peace (see 1 Corinthians 14:33). Therefore, when confusion hits our mind, it's a clear sign enemy interference may be in play. You can find yourself under spiritual attack and not be confused and you can find yourself confused and not be under spiritual attack; but when you deal with strong confusion, it can usually be traced to some expression of witchcraft.

Mental pressure is interesting to study. Mental is anything related to the mind. Mental pressure comes before mind control. Pressure is "the burden of physical or mental stress;" "the application of force to something else in direct contract with it: compression;" "the action of a force upon an imposing force;" "the stress or urgency of matters demanding attention;" "the pressure exerted in every direction by the weight of the atmosphere;" and "a sensation aroused by moderate compression of a body part or surface," according to *Merriam-Webster*.

That's a mouthful. We all face pressures in life. When something becomes unreasonably difficult or forceful, it's usually demonic in nature. When mental stress overtakes you, it could be a Squid Spirit applying force. This kind of mental pressure brings stress and creates a spiritual climate around you that is overwhelming.

Mental pain is "acute mental or emotional stress or suffering: grief." We all deal with emotional stress from life events. But, again, when mental pain overtakes you, it could be the Squid's ink—the Squid's witchcraft—overblowing a situation and making it seem worse than it actually is.

Migraines are a clear physical manifestation of the Squid Spirit. Of course, other factors can cause migraines. Naturally speaking, the Migraine Research Foundation point out that the primary source of a migraine was once thought to be dilation and constriction of blood vessels in the head. Researchers now also point to a neurological disorder that involves nerve pathways and brain chemicals causing migraines.

Just about everyone has headaches. But contrary to popular belief, migraine is not just a bad headache. It's an extremely incapacitating collection of neurological symptoms that usually includes a severe throbbing recurring pain on one side of the head. However, in 1/3 of migraine attacks, both sides are affected. Attacks last between 4 and 72 hours and are often accompanied by one or more of the following disabling symptoms: visual disturbances, nausea, vomiting, dizziness, extreme sensitivity to sound, light, touch and smell, and tingling or numbness in the extremities or face. Of course, everyone is different, and symptoms vary by person and sometimes by attack.[3]

Notice, the foundation calls it an "attack." The organization also says migraines are a moving target, with symptoms changing from one attack to the next and symptoms that can be so debilitating that a doctor visit is required. Migraines can occur naturally, but when the Squid Spirit attacks you could have one of the worst headaches of your life as a physical manifestation of the tentacles—specifically the suckers—applying pressure to your head. Excedrin won't touch it.

Squid's Sneaky Mind Control

Squid, octopus, and mind control spirits are essentially synonymous—though mind control is really a weapon of these marine demons. Mind control is known in the world as brainwashing. God wants to renew your mind by the washing of the water of His Word (see Ephesians 5:26). The Squid Spirit—and its similar octopus spirit—wants to renew your mind with coercive persuasion, thought reform, and thought control.

The mind control's aim is menticide, which *Merriam-Webster* defines as "a systematic and intentional undermining of a person's conscious." Brainwashing uses psychological techniques that block or hinder critical thinking so as to usurp the authority you have over your mind and inject thoughts that defy God's wisdom. These thoughts ultimately work to change how you perceive the world around you and ultimately change your behavior. Mind control wants to turn you into a puppet for the enemy, mindless automatons that can't think straight.

We know that mind control is a real phenomenon, even though brainwashing is debated in scientific circles. Steven Hassan, author of *Combatting Mind Control*, calls it undue influence and defines that influence as "any act of persuasion that overcomes the free will and judgment of another person. People can be unduly influenced by deception, flattery, trickery, coercion, hypnosis, and other techniques."[4]

Eckhardt writes:

> Mind control also gives a person the ability to control the mind of another. Many pastors and church leaders have very powerful mind control spirits. False teachers and cults also use mind control to keep people bound to them. When a person receives deliverance from mind control they are able to think clearly, some for the first time in their life.[5]

The Squid's mind control is spiritual abuse, and I believe many ministries that inflict spiritual abuse on their members are tapping into the Squid Spirit's witchcraft, although clearly the spirit of Jezebel is also a spiritual abuser. Religious cults like Westboro Baptist Church is an extreme example of how a Squid Spirit manifests in the name of Jesus.

ABC's 20/20 television program some years ago exposed the shocking truth about life inside Warren Jeffs' Fundamentalist Latter-Day Saints Church. The cult leader was convicted and jailed for sexual abuse of young girls, yet his 8,000 followers continue to believe he's a persecuted prophet. He's known for ordering married couples to stop having sex and handpicked fifteen men to father all of the cult's children. That's clearly mind control at work.

We see mind control techniques at work in the seven mountains of society. The education mountain is perhaps top among them. Educators are indoctrinating children at young ages to believe lies of all sorts, especially in the area of sexual perversion. In the entertainment mountain, we see what is called "predictive programming," a technique used in Hollywood to prophesy where society is moving.

Consider the science fiction books and movies of the 1960s and then consider our reality today. It's startlingly matching in many ways. In the media mountain, advertising propaganda targets our self-image, making us feel we're not as good as the models on television and in magazines and compelling us to buy merchandise to make us more acceptable.

Squids and Mental Illness

Eckhardt writes, "Mind control works with insanity, mental illness, schizophrenia, intellectualism and a host of others that operate in the mind."[6] Let's break these down one by one. Just as a migraine can be caused by natural factors, so can mental illness. However, I do believe mental illnesses are just as often—if not more often—due to spiritual attacks on the mind as they are chemical imbalances in the body. Again, let's look at the definitions of each of these manifestations of Squid, or mind control, spirits.

According to the American Psychiatric Association:

> Mental illnesses are health conditions involving changes in thinking, emotion or behavior (or a combination of these), according to the American. Mental illnesses are associated with distress and/or problems functioning in social, work or family activities. Mental illness is common. In a given year:

nearly one in five (19 percent) U.S. adults experience some form of mental illness; one in 24 (4.1 percent) has a serious mental illness; one in 12 (8.5 percent) has a substance use disorder. Mental illness is treatable. The vast majority of individuals with mental illness continue to function in their daily lives.[7]

The National Alliance on Mental Illness defines schizophrenia as "a serious mental illness that interferes with a person's ability to think clearly, manage emotions, make decisions and relate to others. It is a complex, long-term medical illness, affecting about 1% of Americans."[8] Symptoms include hallucinations, delusions, being emotionally flat or speaking in a dull, disconnected way, struggling to remember things, organize thoughts and complete tasks. Substance abuse, brain chemistry, environmental factors and genetics are listed as causes in the medical world.

Insanity is officially defined as "a severely disordered state of the mind usually occurring as a specific disorder," according to *Merriam-Webster*. Law.com defines insanity as "mental illness of such a severe nature that a person cannot distinguish fantasy from reality, cannot conduct her/his affairs due to psychosis, or is subject to uncontrollable impulsive behavior."[9]

Intellectualism is an excessive emphasis on abstract or intellectual manners, especially with a lack of proper consideration for emotions; the doctrine that knowledge is wholly or chiefly from pure reason; and the belief that reason is the final principle of realty, according to *Dictionary.com*. Yet the Bible clearly says, *"Trust in the Lord with all your heart and do not lean on your own understanding. In all your ways acknowledge Him, and He will make your paths straight"* (Proverbs 3:5-6).

Speaking about Jesus, the Pharisees said He had a devil and was insane (see John 10:20), which implied He was not in His right mind. Festus accused Paul of being out of his mind (Acts 26:24). When Jesus cast demons out of the insane man in the country of the Gerasenes, the Bible explains, *"The people went out to see what had happened; and they came to Jesus, and found the man from whom the demons had gone out, sitting down at the feet of Jesus, clothed and in his right mind..."* (Luke 8:35). Clearly, insanity and mental illness are tied to demon activity.

When you are under periodic or heavy Squid attack, you can feel like you are losing your mind. Doctors may think you are crazy because tests will show nothing, but your manifestations and complaints are strong. Physicians will blame stress or consider mental illness. Do not allow a doctor to diagnose you with a mental illness when you are under spiritual attack. Likewise, do not take prescription drugs to ease the manifestation of a spiritual attack or you could open the door to the mind control spirit to entrench itself, building a stronghold.

How We Invite Squid In

Yes, we can invite Squid in—but that's not the only way squid and octopus can attack. Squid Spirits can blindside us through no fault of our own or we can be predisposed to these attacks due to bloodline issues. In his *Deliverance and Spiritual Warfare Manual,* Eckhardt writes:

> People can receive mind control spirits through music (rock, jazz, disco, etc.), meditation, reading certain books, drugs and alcohol (or anything that alters the mind and breaks down the hedges) (Ecclesiastes 10:8), passivity, control by another person, exposure of the mind to false teachings, psychology, pornography, etc.[10]

Eckhardt refers to Ecclesiastes 10:8, which reads: *"He who digs a pit may fall into it, and a serpent may bite him who breaks through a wall."* We have to guard our mind gate. Ephesians 4:27 tells us, *"Do not give the devil an opportunity."* Ephesians 4:27 from the New King James Version says, *"nor give place to the devil.*" The Greek word for "place" in this verse is *topos*. It means "place, any portion or space marked off, as it were from surrounding space," according to our lexicon. Metaphorically, it speaks to the "condition or station held by one in any company or assembly opportunity, power, occasion for acting." It's been said if you give the devil an inch, he will take a mile.

Cleary, he's looking for an opportunity. First Peter 5:8 (AMPC) warns, *"Be well balanced (temperate, sober of mind), be vigilant and cautious at all times; for that enemy of yours, the devil, roams around like a lion roaring [in fierce hunger], seeking someone to seize upon and devour."*

Often, we give the enemy an opportunity through our ignorance. Paul speaks in 2 Corinthians 2:11, *"so that no advantage would be taken of us by Satan, for we are not ignorant of his schemes."* Paul is speaking in the context of unforgiveness, but the principle holds true in any context. Satan can take advantage of us through the door of ignorance.

The gates of hell cannot prevail against the Church, but demons incessantly work to enter the gates of our soul, body, relationships, and finances. We are in the world but not of the world, but the spirit of the world works to influence us every day through other people, media, and mind traffic. First John 2:16 tells us, *"For all that is in the world, the lust of the flesh and the lust of the eyes and the boastful pride of life, is not from the Father, but is from the world."*

Living in this world, there is a constant tension—it's a war—for where we will place our affection, what we will look at, what we will listen to, what we will say, who and what we will spend our time with. We must guard our eye gates, our ear gates, and our soul gate.

The soul contains our mind, will, imaginations, emotions, intellect, reasoning. The enemy will press whatever button he can in your soulish realm. John the apostle revealed a key to prosperity in one of his epistles: *"Beloved, I pray that in all respects you may prosper and be in good health, just as your soul prospers"* (3 John 1:2). Soul prosperity is key to combatting spiritual warfare.

We know the battle is in the mind. The devil tries to bend our will to his will through vain imaginations (see 2 Corinthians 10:5). He plays on our emotions. He uses our intellect to dampen our faith. He uses reasonings to lead us into double-mindedness. When our soul is under attack, we have to fight for that prosperity of which John speaks.

The word "prosper" in 1 John 3:1 comes from the Greek word *eujodovw*. According to *The KJV New Testament Greek Lexicon,* it means "to grant a prosperous and expeditious journey, to lead by a direct and easy way; to grant a successful issue, to cause to prosper; to prosper, be successful." When your soul prospers, life is a lot easier and more successful. The enemy knows this, so he works to get through the soul gate, through emotions and mindsets, and will stances like anger, fear, worry, unforgiveness, and the like. If we don't submit our mind, will, imaginations, intellect, and reasoning to the Lord, we are effectively inviting the enemy in to wreak havoc on our prosperity.

Eckhardt points out, "Mind control spirits can also be inherited."[11] A history of mental and emotional breakdown in your family line could come from a generational curse. A generational curse is just what it sounds like: a curse that passes down from generation to generation. There are many books written about generational curses. My goal here is not to offer a dissertation on the topic. But let's look at a few Scriptures about generational curses so you can study this out in the Bible for yourself and understand the basics before we move forward.

> *For I, the Lord your God, am a jealous God, visiting the iniquity of the fathers upon the children to the third and fourth generations of those who hate Me* (Exodus 20:5 NKJV).

> *...by no means clearing the guilty, visiting the iniquity of the fathers upon the children and the children's children to the third and the fourth generation* (Exodus 34:7 NKJV).

> *The Lord is longsuffering and abundant in mercy, forgiving iniquity and transgression; but He by no means clears the guilty, visiting the iniquity of the fathers on the children to the third and fourth generation* (Numbers 14:18 NKJV).

> *...For I, the Lord your God, am a jealous God, visiting the iniquity of the fathers upon the children to the third and fourth generations of those who hate Me* (Deuteronomy 5:9 NKJV).

As you can see, Scripture reveals that the impact of sin passes from generation to generation, hence the phrase "generational curse." So it's not the sin that actually passes through the bloodline, it's the curse that results from the sin—the penalty of sin. Larry Huch, senior pastor of DFW New Beginnings, once put it to me this way:

> "The world says it like this, 'Like father like son.' The Word says it like this, 'The iniquity of the father passes on from generation to generation.' Many times we translate the word 'iniquity' as 'sin.' But it's not the sin that passes on from generation to generation. It's the curse, the penalty. A curse is a spirit that passes from generation to generation until someone finally figures out how to stop it in Jesus' name."

Invasion of the Giant Squid

I believe the natural often parallels the spiritual realm. As we witnessed the overrun of pythons in the Florida Everglades, for example, we saw more Python witchcraft in the atmosphere. If these parallels ring true, then a 2009 *Associated Press* report is especially disturbing:

Thousands of jumbo flying squid, aggressive 5-foot-long sea monsters with razor-sharp beaks and toothy tentacles, have invaded the shallow waters off San Diego, spooking scuba divers and washing up dead on beaches. The so-called Humboldt squid, which can grow up to 100 pounds, are native to the deep waters off Mexico, where they have been known to attack humans.

Scientists are not sure why the squid are swarming off the Southern California coast, but they are concerned. In recent years, small numbers have been spotted from California to Sitka, Alaska, an alarming trend, scientists say. In 2005, a similar invasion off San Diego delighted fishermen and, in 2002, thousands of squid washed up on the beaches. This summer, the wayward squid have also been hauled up by fishermen in waters off Orange County, just north of San Diego.[12]

National Geographic, Discovery Channel and others have also documented this squid invasion—and it's not just in California. Oregon has seen similar invasions—and scientists are concerned.[13]

The Humboldt squid are known in science as "red devils." But the giant squid are another category. Smithsonian calls the giant squid the "dragon of the deep."[14] In legend, this giant squid is called a kraken that took down ships hundreds of years ago—but it's not a legend. Little is known about the giant squid, but the BBC reports: "What is clear is that giant squid are very successful at producing offspring. They seem to live in every ocean, apart from the polar regions, and their population must surely be large if they can satisfy the cravings of so many sperm whales. There are probably millions of them out there..."[15]

Could it be possible the natural realm is manifesting what is going on in the spirit realm with squids and octopuses? I believe so. What's scary in that regard is the reality that researchers have only explored about 5 percent of the ocean. Just as we don't know what really lives in the sea, we likely do not understand the depth of marine demons. But we can rely on the Holy Spirit for revelation as needed.

Endnotes

1. John Eckhardt, *Demon Hit List* (New Kensington, PA: Whitaker House, 2000); https://books.google.com/books?id=tOv1BgAAQ-BAJ&pg=PT31&lpg=PT31&dq=Octopus+and+squid+spirits+having+tentacles;+confusion,+mental+pressure,+mental+pain,+migraine&source=bl&ots=xzrAitjzwL&sig=KH1ubucx-NMqOezjP-M0cQ0cNQV8&hl=en&sa=X&ved=0ahUKEwjyyeaMzMvZAhUL-v1MKHVQyD5sQ6AEIRDAG#v=onepage&q=Octopus%20and%20squid%20spirits%20having%20tentacles%3B%20confusion%2C%20mental%20pressure%2C%20mental%20pain%2C%20migraine&f=false; accessed April 19, 2018.

2. John Eckhardt, *Deliverance and Spiritual Warfare Manual* (Chicago, IL: Crusaders Ministries); http://www.piwcworcester.org/wp-content/uploads/2016/02/Deliverance-and-Spiritual-Warfare-Manual-Eckhardt.pdf; accessed April 19, 2018.

3. Migraine Research Foundation; http://migraineresearchfoundation.org/about-migraine/what-is-migraine/; accessed April 19, 2018.

4. Freedom of Mind Resource Center, "Undue Influence"; https://freedomofmind.com/cult-mind-control/; accessed April 19, 2018.

5. John Eckhardt, *Deliverance and Spiritual Warfare Manual.*

6. Ibid.

7. American Psychiatric Association, "What Is Mental Illness?"; https://www.psychiatry.org/patients-families/what-is-mental-illness; accessed

April 19, 2018.

8. National Alliance on Mental Illness, "Schizophrenia"; https://www.nami.org/learn-more/mental-health-conditions/schizophrenia; accessed April 19, 2018.

9. Law.com, "Insanity"; http://dictionary.law.com/Default.aspx?selected=979; accessed April 19, 2018.

10. John Eckhardt, *Deliverance and Spiritual Warfare Manual.*

11. Ibid.

12. Associated Press, *The New York Times,* "California: Invasion of the Giant Squid!"; http://www.nytimes.com/2009/07/17/science/17brfs-INVASIONOFTH_BRF.html; accessed April 19, 2018.

13. Lori Tobias, "Squid invasion hitting Oregon coast and scientists are concerned, but could there be a silver lining?"; *The Oregonian;* http://www.oregonlive.com/environment/index.ssf/2010/04/squid_invasion_hitting_oregon.html; accessed April 19, 2018.

14. Brian Switek, "The Giant Squid: Dragon of the Deep," *Smithsonian.com;* https://www.smithsonianmag.com/science-nature/the-giant-squid-dragon-of-the-deep-18784038/; accessed April 19, 2018.

15. Melissa Hogenboom, "Are massive squid really the sea monsters of legend?" *BBC,* December 12, 2014; http://www.bbc.com/earth/story/20141212-quest-for-the-real-life-kraken; accessed April 19, 2018.

Chapter 9

SQUEEZING
OUT THE SQUID SPIRIT

S QUID and octopus spirits are fierce predators. In the seas, these creatures don't hesitate to attack humans, using their tentacles to snatch divers from their mission, yank them down forcibly, and disorient them.
The Squid Spirit wants to put a squeeze on you—but you can squeeze it out if
you discern its operations. Part of discerning the squid spirit is understanding
how it attacks.

Naturally speaking, squids can be difficult to discern because they camou-
flage themselves by changing color to match the surrounding environment.
They seem to strike out of nowhere, but they were lying in wait the whole
time, blending into their environment. Squid Spirits work in deception over
the mind, and we see a parallel in the deep.

"Deception occurs even in the deepest parts of oceans, as scientists have
just discovered that a deep-sea squid pretends to be a small animal before
making a deadly attack," ABC Science reports. "It's clearly challenging to
study animal activities that take place so deep in the ocean, but the researchers think it's possible that other squid species and marine molluscs also use
deceptive lures to catch their dinners."[1]

No one I've ever met has immediately discerned a Squid Spirit. It manifests at first like something else—a headache or mind traffic. But make no mistake—sneaky Squid Spirits are often behind what seem like natural circumstances. What makes squids especially dangerous, for example, is their pack mentality. Squids move in squads. That means you're typically not dealing with one squid attacking you—you're dealing with a group. The Humboldt squid is known to move in groups of 1,200.[2] Thank God, one warrior puts a thousand to flight and two can put 10,000 to flight (see Deuteronomy 32:30).

Overwhelming Pressure

The Squid and Octopus Spirits work to undermine God's Word in your life. These marine demons' tentacles are intentional in their pressure to overwhelm the mind. The enemy is expert at coming in like a flood with crushing circumstances and disturbing thoughts that try to drown you in feelings of helplessness and even hopelessness. "Overwhelm" is an enemy I've fought many times over the years, and defeating it starts with understanding what it really is.

Merriam-Webster defines "overwhelm" as to affect (someone) very strongly; to cause (someone) to have too many things to deal with; to defeat (someone or something) completely. Overwhelm also means: upset, overthrow; to cover over completely, submerge; to overcome by superior force or numbers; to overpower in thought or feeling.

Of course, you can be overwhelmed simply from a natural perspective with too much work or too many facts or too much opposition. But the Squid and Octopus Spirit likes to work in our naturally overwhelming circumstances to apply spiritual pressure to the mind with its tentacles and suckers. When that spiritual pressure mounts, too often we look for a way of escape rather than trusting in the Lord for His sufficient grace to meet the situation at hand. Too often we allow Octopus Spirits to oppress us rather than fighting back.

The Squid Spirit also brings overwhelming pain, which often manifests as a migraine-type headache. The Squid attack can also bring on overwhelming infirmities that seem to come out of nowhere and can overwhelm the nervous system to the point where violent shaking and convulsing can manifest. This further overwhelms the mind, which is where the attack really begins. Intense Squid Spirits can make people feel as if they are going insane and may never break free.

Don't feel ashamed in your battle against feeling overwhelmed. David understood these feelings all too well. He once wrote:

> *My heart is severely pained within me, and the terrors of death have fallen upon me. Fearfulness and trembling have come upon me, and horror has* **overwhelmed** *me. So I said, "Oh, that I had wings like a dove! I would fly away and be at rest. Indeed, I would wander far off, and remain in the wilderness. Selah. I would hasten my escape from the windy storm and tempest"* (Psalm 55:4-8 NKJV).

I can't tell you how many times I've wished I could fly away and escape. Yes, this is the same David who ran to the battle line to defeat Goliath without a second (or fearful) thought. And this wasn't the only time David felt overwhelmed. Another time he wrote, *"From the end of the earth I will cry to You, when my heart is overwhelmed; lead me to the rock that is higher than I"* (Psalm 61:2 NKJV). And again, *"When my spirit was overwhelmed within me, then You knew my path..."* (Psalm 142:3 NKJV).

The first step in battling the octopus' overwhelm is to recognize it and acknowledge your situation. Denying feelings of overwhelm won't help you conquer your flesh or the devil. Once you've acknowledged the reality of an overwhelmed heart, you can work with the Holy Spirit to get to the root of these feelings.

What is causing this overwhelm, really? Is the enemy blowing it out of proportion? Is it really as bad as it looks, or is this pressure demonic? Put your circumstances—and your emotions—into perspective. Is there anything you can do right now in the natural to relieve some of the burdens you feel? Ask the Holy Spirit for wisdom in the midst of this trial:

> *My brethren, count it all joy when you fall into various trials, knowing that the testing of your faith produces patience. But let patience have its perfect work, that you may be perfect and complete, lacking nothing. If any of you lacks wisdom, let him ask of God, who gives to all liberally and without reproach, and it will be given to him. But let him ask in faith, with no doubting, for he who doubts is like a wave of the sea driven and tossed by the wind. For let not that man suppose that he will receive anything from the Lord; he is a double-minded man, unstable in all his ways* (James 1:2-8 NKJV).

God Is Not Overwhelmed

While you wait for this pure wisdom that comes from above, meditate on Jesus. Get your mind off the overwhelming circumstances and onto the Word of God. Pray for grace, strength, and whatever else you feel you need from Father in the moment. Remind yourself of His promises. Here are a few I like to keep in mind when overwhelm tries to wreak havoc on my soul:

> *The Lord is my strength and my shield; my heart trusted in Him, and I am helped; Therefore my heart greatly rejoices, and with my song I will praise Him* (Psalm 28:7 NKJV).

I can do all things through Christ who strengthens me (Philippians 4:13 NKJV).

God is our refuge and strength, a very present help in trouble. Therefore we will not fear, even though the earth be removed, and though the mountains be carried into the midst of the sea; though its waters roar and be troubled, though the mountains shake with its swelling (Psalm 46:1-3 NKJV).

Be still, and know that I am God... (Psalm 46:10 NKJV).

And remember David. When he was overwhelmed with Saul hunting him down and with Absalom trying to overtake his kingdom and with his baby son dying and with even his own sin, he always turned to God. Here is one of his prayers for help in troubling times that you may want to pray for yourself:

I cry aloud with my voice to the Lord. I make supplication with my voice to the Lord. I pour out my complaint before Him; I declare my trouble before Him. When my spirit was overwhelmed within me, You knew my path. In the way where I walk they have hidden a trap for me. Look to the right and see; for there is no one who regards me; There is no escape for me; no one cares for my soul.

I cried out to You, O Lord; I said, "You are my refuge, my portion in the land of the living. Give heed to my cry, for I am brought very low; deliver me from my persecutors, for they are too strong for me. Bring my soul out of prison, so that I may give thanks to Your name; the righteous will surround me, for You will deal bountifully with me" (Psalm 142).

Amen!

Conquering the Squid Spirit

After this Squid Spirit attacked my friend, I went to her home to help her battle it. The attack was severe, but when I laid hands on her and commanded the Squid to be bound, the most violent symptoms would cease. Of course, when you stand in the gap, you often take a hit. That Squid Spirit started stalking me. I ended up with a migraine during the battle—a manifestation of that mind control spirit—and was attacked in my mind for days afterward.

Fear can open the door to a Squid Spirit. Of course, unforgiveness is an open door for the enemy. But let's face it, the enemy doesn't need an open door to attack. He can strike when we least expect it, which is why we're to live in a battle-ready state and walk with the Spirit of God who can warn us of impending attacks.

According to John Eckhardt's book *Deliverance and Spiritual Warfare Manual*, "These spirits hate the anointing of the forehead with oil, and this is helpful in binding them. Also anointing the top, back, and sides (temples) of the head is sometimes necessary."[3] Eckhardt teaches the squid's tentacles need to be severed from the minds because it breaks mind control's power and speeds the deliverance. Psalm 129:4 assures us, *"The Lord is righteous; He has cut in two the cords of the wicked."*

We can sever the squid's tentacles by declaring, "I sever the squid's tentacles, in Jesus' name." However, we must also employ the Sword of the Spirit, which is the Word of God. We can declare we have the mind of Christ (see 1 Corinthians 2:16). We can cast down imaginations that the attack will never end, the pain will never go, and the overwhelm will never break (see 2 Corinthians 10:5). We can gird up the loins of our mind (see 1 Peter 1:13). We can choose to obey Philippians 4:8-9:

> *Finally, brethren, whatever is true, whatever is honorable, whatever is right, whatever is pure, whatever is lovely, whatever is of good repute, if there is any excellence and if anything*

worthy of praise, dwell on these things. The things you have learned and received and heard and seen in me, practice these things, and the God of peace will be with you.

I've discovered that it's difficult to fight the squid alone. That is likely due to the squads of squids deployed against the believer's mind. When you discern a squid attack, wisdom calls for reinforcements. The good news here is a squid's tentacles do not grow back once severed. If you get discernment that a Squid Spirit is attacking you, repent for any known open doors, grab some intercessors, and get that sneaky stalker with its manipulating suckers off your mind! Sever the tentacles, in the name of Jesus, and walk free.

After that Squid skirmish, I was reading Richard Ing's book *Spiritual Warfare,* and he described the spirit of mind control as often seen as a giant squid with ten tentacles that stick into brains or cover heads. He said it sometimes looks like a brown cylinder or dark brown bands that cover someone's head and body. He went on to discuss a vision he had one night after praying about this Squid Spirit:

> I found myself floating a few hundred feet above a park-like clearing. I saw a grassy area surrounded by trees. In the center of the clearing, someone held a large bunch of balloons of various colors. In the second scene, I saw a man with a wide, ark brown band around his head and around his body. The bands appeared almost black in color and looked like the metal bands that hold wooden barrels together. Suddenly something cut or broke the bands, and they fell off. The man smiled. Immediately, I found myself above the park again. Then, I saw the balloons floating freely up towards and beyond me. It seemed as if the person holding the balloons had let them go. They floated into the heavens.

The very next day, I sat in church discussing the spirit of mind control. The assistant pastor shared that he had received a vision the night before in which he found himself bound up with dark brown bands around his head and body. We went after the spirit of mind control that night, and a number of people received deliverance from that spirit.[4]

Amen, deliverance belongs to you! People may think you are all-out crazy if you mention a Squid Spirit. I've had mean-spirited Christians who are ignorant of the reality of the spiritual warfare world persecute me for exposing this demon. In fact, they've even made posters of me with squids over my face and printed T-shirts that claim "No squid spirit formed against me shall prosper," quoting 2 Tentacles as the verse. I would advise never to mock the things of the spirit because they are more real than what you can see. Many times when we mock things in the spirit we don't understand, we open ourselves up to attack. I pray my persecutors never meet with a Squid Spirit.

A Prayer to Squeeze Out the Squid Spirit

Father, in the name of Jesus, I ask for forgiveness and deliverance from the Squid Spirit's ties that bind. I repent for opening the door to mind control spirits by entertainment I've viewed or other sources of wickedness I've allowed through my eye gates and ear gates. Forgive me, in Jesus' name.

Now, I break every curse of mental illness, including depression, anxiety, bipolar, manic depression, multiple personalities, insanity, and schizophrenia in my family line. I say I have the mind of Christ and think His thoughts and His thoughts only. I plead the blood of Jesus over my mind. Help me to recognize the inroads of the Squid Spirit's mind control and resist it at its onset.

I take authority over the Squid Spirit and Octopus Spirit's assignment against my mind and my nervous system. I command Squid and Octopus to loose me, in Jesus' name. O severe the tentacles of these marine demons.

I extract the Squid and Octopus' suckers, in the name of Christ. I extract myself from this strong, multifaceted grip of the enemy and demolish its stronghold in my mind and over my body, in Jesus' name. Thank You, Lord, for setting me free from mind-binding, mind-control, Squid and Octopus influences and attacks, in Jesus' name.

Endnotes

1. Jennifer Viegas, "Deep sea squid lure prey for attack," *ABC Science,* August 28, 2013; http://www.abc.net.au/science/articles/2013/08/28/3835642.htm; accessed April 20, 2018.

2. Rob Harris, "Why Are Squid Dangerous?" http://animals.mom.me/squid-dangerous-5446.html; accessed April 20, 2018.

3. John Eckhardt, *Deliverance and Spiritual Warfare Manual;* https://books.google.com/books?id=abDIAwAAQBAJ&pg=PA230&lpg=PA230&dq=These+spirits+hate+the+anointing+of+the+forehead+with+oil,+and+this+is+helpful+in+binding+them.+Also+anointing+the+top,+back,+and+sides+(temples)+of+the+head+is+sometimes+necessary.%E2%80%9D&source=bl&ots=oKUtqinRGr&sig=aJziIi2pUy2aiPGL94ekQStcJRE&hl=en&sa=X-&ved=0ahUKEwiSuK--rtDZAhXhpVkKHZjmAQoQ6AEIKTAA#v=onepage&q=These%20spirits%20hate%20the%20anointing%20of%20the%20forehead%20with%20oil%2C%20and%20this%20is%20helpful%20in%20binding%20them.%20Also%20anointing%20the%20top%2C%20back%2C%20and%20sides%20(temples)%20of%20the%20head%20is%20sometimes%20necessary.%E2%80%9D&f=false

4. Richard Ing, *Spiritual Warfare* (New Kensington, PA: Whitaker House, 1996), 223-224.

Chapter 10

REJECTING
THE SPIRIT OF RAHAB

W HEN you think of Rahab, you probably think of the harlot in the Book of Joshua who hid the Israelite spies from enemy harm (see Joshua 2). The Messiah was birthed through this Rahab's bloodline. But when we speak of the Rahab Spirit, we're not talking about this celebrated heroine who played a key role in Israel's crossing over into the Promised Land—we're talking about a dragon that rises up in times of crossing over.

We find mention of this spirit in Isaiah 51:9-10:

> *Awake, awake, put on strength, O arm of the Lord; awake as in the days of old, the generations of long ago. Was it not You who cut Rahab in pieces, who pierced the dragon? Was it not You who dried up the sea, the waters of the great deep; who made the depths of the sea a pathway for the redeemed to cross over?*

Although some theologians and translations point to this Rahab as a symbol of Egypt and others contend this a mythological creature, its idea of the dragon signifies something greater than a nation or a myth. And, again, we know that gods or spirits in the world of mythology are many times actual demon entities that wreak havoc in the earth. Rahab is one such demon—a marine demon that attacks during times of crossing over.

Rahab is clearly associated with a dragon spirit in Isaiah 51:9-10. *Elliot's Commentary for English Readers* suggests Egypt invoked a god named Ra, from the Egyptian Book of the Dead. Isaiah seems to be asking God to raise up against the oppression upon the Israelite people like He did against the Egyptians.

In the New International Version, Job 9:13 speaks of Rahab: *"God does not restrain his anger; even the cohorts of Rahab cowered at his feet."* In the New King James Version, Rahab is translated "proud helpers" but some Bible commentators translate it as "helpers of pride." *Pulpit Commentary* reveals:

> *Rahab in this passage, and also in Job 26:12, as well us in Isaiah 51:9, seems to be used as the proper name of some great power of evil. Such a power was recognized in the mythology of Egypt, under the names of Set (or Typhon) and of Apophia, the great serpent, continually represented as pierced by Horus.... In the earlier Aryan myths there is a similar personification of evil in Vitre, called Dasiya, "the Destroyer," and at perpetual enmity with Indra and Agni.... The Babylonians and Assyrians had a tradition of a great "war in heaven"...carried on by seven spirits, who were finally reduced to subjection.*

> *All these seem to be distorted reminiscences of that great conflict, whereof the only trustworthy account is the one contained in the Revelation of St. John, "There was war in heaven: Michael and his angels fought against the dragon; and the dragon fought and his angels"—the "helpers" of the present passage—"and prevailed not; neither was their place found any more in heaven"* (Revelation 12:7-8).

Job, it seems, had inherited one of such traditions, one in which the power of evil was known as Rahab, "the Proud One"; and he means here to say that God holds not only men in subjection, but also beings much more powerful than man, as Rahab and his helpers, who had rebelled and made war on God, and been east down from heaven, and were now prostrate under God's feet."

Indeed, the name Rahab means "proud and quarrelsome, according to *Hitchcock's Bible Names Dictionary*. *Smith's Bible Dictionary* defines Rahab as "signifying fierceness, insolence and pride. *The International Standard Bible Encyclopedia* defines Rahab as "storm" and "arrogance." The encyclopedia also reveals the Talmud in Baha' Bathra' speaks of Rahab as "master of the sea."

Hitchcock's secondary definition is large and extended. That comes from the root verb that "means to be or become large or wide" and is used to indicate the spaciousness of land or territory, according to *Abarim Publications' Biblical Name Vault*.

NOBSE Study Bible Name List connects the name Rahab with violence. *Jones' Dictionary of Old Testament Proper Names* defines Rahab as "insolence." *Abarim* reports *HAW Theological Wordbook of the Old Testament* and *BDB Theological Dictionary* offer an original meaning of "storming against something or someone."

Are Dragons Real?

Rahab—the dragon—is raging against many in the church. The word "dragon" in Isaiah 51:9-10 means "dragon, serpent, sea monster, dinosaur, river monster, venomous snake," according to *The KJV Old Testament Hebrew Lexicon*. The most accurate definition, though, is dragon in the context of the Rahab marine demon.

We've seen dragons in pop culture. You might recall the Peter, Paul, and Mary's song about *Puff the Magic Dragon*, who lived by the sea in a land called Honahlee. We see dragons in *Shrek*, *Pete's Dragon*, *Aladdin*, *Sleeping Beauty*,

The Hobbit, and many other movies. We see television shows, like *Power Rangers, Ninja Turtles,* and *The Chronicles of Narnia* highlight dragons. We see dragons in comic books, dragons in games—Dungeons & Dragons being a prime example—and dragon toys. We see dragons in literature, dragons in theme parks, and sports teams named after dragons.

We see dragons in folklore and dragons in Greek mythology. The list of dragons is seemingly endless. Is there a running theme that offers any revelation into the Rahab Spirit? There's Aido Wedo, known as the Rainbow Serpent of Dahomey mythology. This religion helped form Voodoo as we know it today. Voodoo stems from African polytheism and ancestor worship typically found in Haiti. Then there's Apalala, a mythical river dragon that converted to Buddhism. Slavic mythology has a fire-spitting dragon known as "snake son of the mountain" with three heads and wings.

Many are familiar with the Chinese dragon from eating in Chinese restaurants. This mythical creature appears as a snake with four legs and is thought to carry power over water, rainfall, typhoons, and floods. Sounds like a water spirit, right? Dragon worship in China dates back to 4700 BC. Also associated with water, Japanese dragons are typically seen as good wish-granters. In Korea you find the Imoogi, or the "great lizard," a homeless ocean dragon. European dragon folklore tends to find heroes conquering dragons. Some have wings. Some breathe fire. Some have fiery tails.

These representations of dragons may look and sound different, but they are anything but cute. Both *Dictionary.com* and *Merriam-Webster* define a dragon as a mythical creature. But dragons—essentially winged snakes that breathe fire—are no myth. Answers in Genesis provides this commentary:

> Genesis 1 tells us that on Day Five of Creation God created great "sea creatures" [Hebrew word *tanninim,* a word we'll explore below] and flying creatures, so this would have included swimming pliosaurs and flying pterodactyls, which we would call dragons. God made land animals, including

dinosaurs and other land dragons, on Day Six, the day He created man. So man lived among these awesome creatures from the beginning. Does the Bible mention dragons? Used multiple times in Scripture, the Hebrew word tannin is defined by *The Enhanced Brown-Driver-Briggs Hebrew and English Lexicon* as "serpent, dragon, sea-monster." It likely refers to certain reptiles, including giant marine creatures and serpentine land animals.... Dragons are real—created creatures, some of which terrorized in the waters and others that roved the land and air.[1]

What the Bible Says About Dragons

Not to be ignored, the word "dragon" appears in the King James Version of the Bible twenty-one times. Dragons are real and dragon spirits are real—and they are terrorizers despite a move in the 21st century to paint dragons as benevolent helpers. Although Leviathan and Behemoth could symbolically fall into the dragon category, Rahab is most directly connected in Scripture to the dragon. Let's look at what the Bible says about dragons.

Nehemiah 2:13 (KJV) speaks of the *"dragon well."* What does this mean? The word "dragon" in this verse comes from the Hebrew word *tanniyn*. According to *The KJV Old Testament Hebrew Lexicon*, it means dragon, serpent, sea monster, river monster, dinosaur, or venomous snake.

Dean Stanley suggests that *"the dragon well"* is the spring known generally as *"the pool of Siloam,"* and that the legend, which describes the intermittent flow of the Siloam water as produced by the opening and closing of a dragon's mouth, had already sprung up.[2] *Gill's Exposition of the Entire Bible* contends the well—which is associated with water—is "so called from its winding about, just as a crooked winding river is called serpentine; though some think here stood an image of a dragon, either in wood, or stone, or brass, out of the mouth of which the water flowed from the well; and others, that since the desolations of Jerusalem, serpents or dragons had their abode here."

Job explained, *"I am a brother to dragons, and a companion to owls"* (Job 30:29 KJV). *Jamieson-Fausset-Brown Bible Commentary* suggests Job was speaking of uttering "dismal screams" and "living amidst solitudes (the emblem of desolation)." This indicates dragons were not benevolent wish-granters that modern filmmakers have painted them to be—and also indicates dragons were very real.

Jeremiah also referred to dragons over and again in the Bible book that carries his name. God said He would make Jerusalem a *"den of dragons"* (Jeremiah 9:11 KJV). Clearly, this was not a desirable fate for Jerusalem. This is a negative context. Jeremiah 10:22 again speaks of this den of dragons. A den is a place where wild animals rest, live, take refuge, or hide. Jeremiah 49:33 and 51:37 speak of the dwelling of dragons.

The Dragon Attacks the Prophetic Anointing

Jeremiah 14:6 speaks of snuffing up the wind like dragons. This is an especially telling verse. *Gill's* reveals dragons are hot by nature and open their mouths "not only to draw in air, but even birds flying." But the word "wind" in that verse is the Hebrew *ruwach*. According to *The KJV Old Testament Hebrew Lexicon*, this speaks of the wind, breath, mind, and spirit. It speaks of the wind of heaven, courage, and the prophetic spirit. Rahab works to knock the wind out of you, squash your courage, and quench your prophetic flow.

Ruwach is also used for the Spirit of God, "as inspiring ecstatic state of prophecy, as impelling prophet to utter instruction or warning, imparting warlike energy and executive and administrative power, as endowing men with various gifts, as energy of life...." The dragon stands against the Holy Spirit, oppressing its targets so it does not press in to manifest the prophetic gifts, the warlike energy, or the power of God.

Psalm 44:19 (KJV) speaks of being broken and covered with the shadow of death in the place of dragons, which reveals the waters in which dragons dwell as harmful and even deadly. Jeremiah 51:34 points to being swallowed up like a dragon. The Hebrew word for "swallow" in this verse is *bala*. The *NASB Old Testament Hebrew Lexicon* defines *bala* as "to swallow down, swallow up, engulf, eat up." This word is translated in other Bible verses as "brought to confusion," "confound," "consume," "destroy," or "ruin." Like serpents, dragons were thought to swallow their prey whole. This speaks to Rahab's overwhelming witchcraft.

Isaiah offered many prophetic parallels to dragons. Isaiah 34:13 and 35:7 both speak of the inhabitations of dragons and paints a bleak picture. *Gill's* suggests this means, "literally, as it figuratively had been the seat of the old dragon, the devil, and of the beast to whom the dragon gave his power, seat, and authority; and who, though he looked like a lamb, spoke like a dragon." Isaiah 27:1 tells us there is coming a day when the Lord will slay the dragon that is in the sea.

Satan Himself Is Depicted as a Dragon

Of course, satan himself is associated with a dragon in the end times, signaling the rise of the dragon in the last of the last days to prevent the ultimate crossing over. Revelation 12:3-4 (KJV) says:

> *And there appeared another wonder in heaven; and behold a great red dragon, having seven heads and ten horns, and seven crowns upon his heads. And his tail drew the third part of the stars of heaven, and did cast them to the earth: and the dragon stood before the woman which was ready to be delivered, for to devour her child as soon as it was born.*

Of the dragon, *Matthew Henry's Concise Commentary* says:

A dragon is a known emblem of Satan, and his chief agents, or those who govern for him on earth, at that time the pagan empire of Rome, the city built upon seven hills. As having ten horns, divided into ten kingdoms. Having seven crowns, representing seven forms of government. As drawing with his tail a third part of the stars in heaven, and casting them down to the earth; persecuting and seducing the ministers and teachers.

Revelation 12:7-10 (KJV) tells us:

And there was war in heaven: Michael and his angels fought against the dragon; and the dragon fought and his angels, and prevailed not; neither was their place found any more in heaven. And the great dragon was cast out, that old serpent, called the Devil, and Satan, which deceiveth the whole world: he was cast out into the earth, and his angels were cast out with him. And I heard a loud voice saying in heaven, Now is come salvation, and strength, and the kingdom of our God, and the power of his Christ: for the accuser of our brethren is cast down, which accused them before our God day and night.

"Dragon" in this Scripture comes from the Hebrew word *drakon. The KJV New Testament Greek Lexicon* defines this word as "a dragon, a great serpent, a name for Satan." The same serpent that plagued the Garden of Eden in the beginning grew into a great dragon in the end times.

Rahab Attacks While Crossing Over

Dragons attack at a time of crossing over—or giving birth. The most striking, direct example is found in Revelation 12 after the war in heaven with Michael and his angels against the dragon and his demons. Revelation 12:13-17 (AMPC) reads:

> *And when the dragon saw that he was cast down to the earth, he went in pursuit of the woman who had given birth to the male Child. But the woman was supplied with the two wings of a giant eagle, so that she might fly from the presence of the serpent into the desert (wilderness), to the retreat where she is to be kept safe and fed for a time, and times, and half a time (three and one-half years, or 1,260 days).*
>
> *Then out of his mouth the serpent spouted forth water like a flood after the woman, that she might be carried off with the torrent. But the earth came to the rescue of the woman, and the ground opened its mouth and swallowed up the stream of water which the dragon had spouted from his mouth.*
>
> *So then the dragon was furious (enraged) at the woman, and he went away to wage war on the remainder of her descendants—[on those] who obey God's commandments and who have the testimony of Jesus Christ [and adhere to it and [a] bear witness to Him].*

John the apostle recorded a fascinating account. Rahab attacks during times of transition or giving birth. How does the dragon attack? One strategy is persecution. Revelation 12:13 says *"he persecuted the woman."* The word "persecution" in this verse comes from the Greek word *dioko*. Our lexicon defines this as "to make or run or flee, put to flight, drive away." Rahab wants you to run from God's transitions and new births in your life—to abort or abandon what He has called you to be or do.

Another definition describes Rahab's portion—"to run swiftly in order to catch a person or thing, to run after, to press on, to pursue." Rahab is in hot pursuit of those transitioning into something according to God's leading for their lives. *Dioko* also means "in any way whatever to harass, trouble, molest one." Rahab is a harassing spirit. It will not just try once to stop you from crossing over. This harassing spirit is relentless.

Isaiah 43:20 says there is coming a day when the dragons will honor God. Thankfully, Jesus Christ will bring the dragon and every spirit to defeat—and every knee will bow, including the Rahab Spirit, at His Second Coming. He will break the heads of the dragons in the waters (see Psalm 74:13 KJV). Psalm 148:7 (KJV) exclaims, *"Praise the Lord from the earth, ye dragons, and all deeps...."* All creatures will praise Him. Until then, we need not be ignorant to this marine demon. And we must remember, *"Thou shalt tread upon the lion and adder: the young lion and the dragon shalt thou trample under feet"* (Psalm 91:13).

Endnotes

1. Answers in Genesis, "Dragons: Fact or Fable?"; https://answersingenesis.org/dinosaurs/dragon-legends/dragons-fact-or-fable/; accessed April 20, 2018.

2. Arthur P. Stanley, *Lectures on the History of the Jewish Church,* Third Series, 125.

Chapter 11

RISING UP
AGAINST RAHAB

RAHAB is attacking, but are we discerning this dragon attack? The reality is you won't rise up against a spiritual rampage you don't recognize. A Rahab attack isn't always readily realized, especially in a spiritual warfare world that focuses predominantly on Jezebel and witchcraft. But Rahab is raging in the spirit realm and will continue rising in the last days.

Rick Ridings, leader of the 24-Hour House of Prayer in Jerusalem, saw Rahab in the spirit. He says he had a vision of a fire-breathing dragon circling the Temple Mount in Jerusalem. During a meeting in Israel with Chuck Pierce, founder of Glory of Zion Ministries, he explained Rahab's horrifying attack: When flames came out of the dragon's mouth, violence was released.[1] Remember, one of the meanings of Rahab is violence.

In a second vision, Ridings saw an imprisoned dragon shrieking and attempting to break out of its dungeon. He says he saw demon spirits coming out of its mouth to incite terror in the prison in which he was caged. Ridings felt the strategy was to ask the Lord to give a "gag and restraining order" to silence the dragon.[2]

What does the voice of the dragon sound like? Snakes hiss. Giraffes are mute. Antelopes snort. Bats screech. Cats meow. Bees buzz. What does the voice of a dragon sound like? Scripture gives us some insight. Micah 1:8 (KJV) tells us dragons wail. Wail means to express sorrow, mourning, or to complain. When a Rahab spirit attacks your mind, it will bring sorrow, mourning, and complaints against God, people, and circumstances.

Dragons "snuff up," according to Jeremiah 14:6. The Hebrew word here is *shawaf. The KJV Old Testament Hebrew Lexicon* translates as "to gasp, pant, pant after, long for, breathe heavily" and "to be eager for; to thirst for one's blood" and "to crush, trample and trample upon." This idea translates as devour or swallow up in some Scriptures. One of the ways Rahab swallows up believers is through strife.

Rahab's Voice of Strife

Rahab's proud voice introduces strife into your life. Strife is a weapon of the enemy because it opens the door to mass attack. James 3:16 (KJV) warns us clearly: *"For where envying and strife is, there is confusion and every evil work."* And the Amplified Bible Classic version really draws it out: *"For wherever there is jealousy (envy) and contention (rivalry and selfish ambition), there will also be confusion (unrest, disharmony, rebellion) and all sorts of evil and vile practices."*

I was once in leadership at a church that was always at war. Spiritual warriors were always in combat with this, that, or the other spirit, and never seemed to be able to close the door. The truth was, many had yielded to a garden variety spirit of strife. Indeed, you could see this spirit of strife manifest on international outreaches and community events alike. There was an angry undercurrent woven into the fabric of the church.

Oh, how it must have grieved the Holy Spirit to see men of God belittling one another and sisters in Christ contending to have their way instead of preferring one another in honor. There was no discernment among the leadership about the true root of the warfare because the staff had grieved the One who offers the gift of discerning of spirits.

This church opened the door to the principalities and powers that were assaulting it by refusing to resist strife's whispers. That spirit of strife stymied the growth of the church and its people, many who left complaining, "There's no love in this church." I dare say the spirit of strife helped lead many into deception as they were always buffeting the air against principalities and powers but never repenting for the pride in their own hearts. They didn't see it. They didn't want to see it.

Strife spreads like wildfire. And it's not always so obvious as bickering on the worship team, screaming in staff meetings, or behind-the-door brow beatings. You may never see these things going on if you aren't in the "inner circle." Politically correct church leaders are experts at masking an angry spirit. Or maybe you do see it. And maybe you see it in your own heart.

So what does strife look like and what causes it? Where you see power struggles and exertion of superiority, you can't automatically blame Jezebel. Strife is the likely motivator. When you see arguing or contending over anything, it's not always rebellion. Strife is typically lurking. When you see double standards where one escapes correction for a major offense and another is sternly rebuked for a minor offense, strife could be at the root.

Beloved, strife is an abomination to God (see Proverbs 6:16-19). Strife affects the anointing and the flow of the Holy Spirit (see Psalm 133:1-3). Strife grieves the Holy Spirit (see Ephesians 4:30). Strife destroys relationships (see Proverbs 17:9). Strife is rooted in anger (see Proverbs 29:22), hatred (see Proverbs 10:12), pride (see Proverbs 13:10), and a quarrelsome self-seeking spirit (see Galatians 5:14-18; Luke 22:24-27). James put it this way:

> *Where do wars and fights come from among you? Do they not come from your desires for pleasure that war in your members? You lust and do not have. You murder and covet and cannot*

obtain. You fight and war. Yet you do not have because you do not ask. You ask and do not receive, because you ask amiss, that you may spend it on your pleasures (James 4:1-3 NKJV).

It was James who also said this:

But if ye have bitter envying and strife in your hearts, glory not, and lie not against the truth. This wisdom descendeth not from above, but is earthly, sensual, devilish. For where envying and strife is, there is confusion and every evil work (James 3:14-16 KJV).

Let me repeat what James wrote so you don't miss it—where envying and strife is, there is confusion and every evil work. Rahab speaks with a voice of strife to open the door to other spirits to attack. Lock the door behind you.

Rahab's Contemptuous Speech

Rahab speaks with a fierce voice of insolence—and insolent means insulting, overbearing, bold, contemptuous speech or conduct. Contemptuous means, "manifesting, feeling or expressing deep hatred or disappointment: feeling or showing contempt." That's a strong voice!

Rahab is a scoffer. Scoffers jeer, mock, and treat you with contempt. The Bible has plenty to say about the scoffer. Relying on Scripture to discern the scoffer's voice can help us discern a Rahab attack, either against our mind or through someone, this water spirit is influencing.

Someone under Rahab's influence will *"sit in the seat of scoffers"* (Psalm 1:1). Proverbs 24:21 tells us "Proud," "Haughty," "Scoffer," are his names, who acts with insolent pride. And Proverbs 24:9 tells us, *"The devising of folly is sin, and the scoffer is an abomination to men."* Strong words! An abomination is something that is disgusting to the Lord; it's something God hates.

Keep in mind the words of the Preacher in the context of the severity of Rahab's disgust in the eyes of God:

> *There are six things which the Lord hates, yes, seven which are an abomination to Him: Haughty eyes, a lying tongue, and hands that shed innocent blood, a heart that devises wicked plans, feet that run rapidly to evil, a false witness who utters lies, and one who spreads strife among brothers* (Proverbs 6:17).

Rahab certainly falls into this category.

Keep in mind one of *The KJV Old Testament Hebrew Lexicon's* definitions of the Hebrew word for scoffer is "interpreter." The Rahab Spirit interprets everything through pride. Another definition is "ambassador." In a figurative sense, Rahab not only scoffs but leads the charge in opposing God's ideas for people, cities, and nations. The dragon stands against God's will—and God Himself (see Psalm 14:1).

It's difficult to win over someone under Rahab's influence. Proverbs 15:12 informs us, *"A scoffer does not love one who reproves him, he will not go to the wise."* And we'll see more people give way to this spirit in the last days. Second Peter 3:3 offers a sober warning: *"Know this first of all, that in the last days mockers will come with their* mocking, following after their own lusts."

But this spirit cannot stand forever. Isaiah 29:20 assures us, *"For the ruthless will come to an end and the scorner will be finished, indeed all who are intent on doing evil will be cut off."* We know *"Judgments are prepared for scoffers"* (Proverbs 19:29). When we drive out the scoffer, contention goes with this spirit (see Proverbs 22:10). We won't see Rahab exterminated until Jesus comes back, but we can pray the Lord will help those under its influence to drive that spirit out of their thinking.

Rahab's Strong Storms

Where you find Rahab, you find storms. In fact, the word "Rahab" in Hebrew means "storm" and "sea monster," according to the *NAS Exhaustive Concordance*. Rahab is an arrogant voice that stirs up storms in your life. It storms against your mind, looking for agreement. Rahab brings dread like a storm and calamity like a whirlwind (see Proverbs 1:27).

Consider the very meaning of storm. Some *Merriam-Webster* definitions of storm is "a disturbed or agitated state; storms of emotion; a sudden or violent commotion; a tumultuous outburst; a violent assault or a defended position." Remember, again, that Rahab brings violence.

I've learned over the years that sudden storms will come, sometimes at the hand of Rahab. This is our reality: *"The thief does not come, except to steal and kill and destroy. I* [Jesus] *came that they may have life, and that they may have it more abundantly"* (John 10:10). In Rahab attacks—in stormy times—we have to remember to choose abundant life. We have to remember the power of death and life are in the tongue (see Proverbs 18:21). We have to choose whether we will believe the Rahab's haughty lies or believe our Savior's truth.

That means knowing the Word of God. Paul admonished Timothy to, *"Be diligent to present yourself approved to God, a worker who does not need to be ashamed, rightly dividing the word of truth"* (2 Timothy 2:15 NKJV). And Revelation 12:11 tells us how to overcome Rahab—by the blood of the Lamb, the word of our testimony, and selflessness.

During Rahab's attacks and storms, our minds and bodies get worn down. Proverbs 24:10 (NKJV) warns us, *"If you faint in the day of adversity, your strength is small."* We must build ourselves up by spending more time with God when sudden storms try to overtake us. We need enduring spirits—strength in our inner self. Isaiah 40:31 (KJV) says, *"They that wait upon the Lord shall renew their strength; they shall mount up with wings as eagles, they shall run and not be weary, and they shall walk and not faint."* Psalm 107:29

assures us the Lord causes the storm to be still and that He is a refuge from the storm (see Isaiah 25:4).

You have to determine in your heart ahead of time that you will not quit during Rahab's sudden and violent storms, because everything in you will drive you toward throwing in the towel. The truth is, no weapon formed against you can prosper (see Isaiah 54:17). Rahab's weapons will form and may appear to be prospering, but the enemy only has the authority in your life that you give him through fear, doubt, unbelief, and surrender. We need to surrender to the will of God and not the will of Rahab's fire-breathing attacks. Pick up your weapons and fight—and surround yourself with people who will fight with you. We're not called to fight alone.

The Ultimate Key to Defeating Rahab

Rahab can be difficult to resist because, at its core, it's a spirit of pride. We all know we can't battle Rahab or any other demon in the flesh, yet the temptation is to rely on the flesh in warfare in subtle ways. We can take pride in our spiritual warfare skills. But it's not just pride in our warfare skills that can hinder our effectiveness in destroying strongholds. It's pride in any area of our life.

We all have a measure of pride in our carnal nature. But when the Holy Spirit is dealing with us about pride in some area—or when we see our own pride and don't cry out for the grace of humility—we're walking in sheer disobedience. The Bible says we are to have a *"readiness to revenge all disobedience, when your obedience is fulfilled"* (2 Corinthians 10:6 KJV). I believe the more we seek to walk in obedience to the Word of God, the more effective we'll be in spiritual warfare against Rahab and all other spirits.

So we return once again to the admonition of James:

> *He gives more grace. Therefore He says: "God resists the proud,*
> *but gives grace to the humble." Therefore submit to God. Resist*
> *the devil and he will flee from you. Draw near to God and He*
> *will draw near to you. Cleanse your hands, you sinners; and*
> *purify your hearts, you double-minded* (James 4:6-8 NKJV).

In our flesh, we're no match for the devil. We need the power of the Holy Spirit to back up our authority in Christ to root out, pull down, destroy, throw down, build, and plant. We can't drive demons into obedience to the Word of God when we're blatantly disobeying the Word of God in any area, whether it's walking in pride or some other sin.

Before you engage in spiritual warfare against Rahab, examine your heart, and take the time to break agreement with the enemy, repent before God and ask for His guidance. It could be that you've opened the door to the spiritual enemies that are attacking you and that simply renouncing agreement with them will stop the attack.

Really think about it. Are you wailing and complaining against God? Are you sowing discord? Are you scoffing?

When we're sure our hands and hearts are clean, we can enter spiritual warfare with confidence but not arrogance. We can be confident that God will lead us into triumph over our enemies if we lean and depend on Him and not on carnal weapons or pride. Amen.

A Prayer to Send Rahab Running

Father, I come to You with a heart of repentance for allowing Rahab to influence my thinking in any way, shape, or form. Forgive me for entertaining or sowing strife and discord, which is an abomination to You. Forgive me for scoffing, in Jesus' name.

I break any and all agreement with the haughty Rahab Spirit, whether known or unknown. Show me my wicked ways so I can repent thoroughly. Examine my heart and purge anything that hinders love, in Jesus' name.

I take authority over Rahab's attacks against my mind and body. I silence the voice of the wailing mourner who works to depress my soul and embitter me against You and others. I forgive those who have hurt me and break the powers of Rahab's storms against my life, my family, my finances, my friendships, and my health. I stand against Rahab and command this wicked spirit to cease and desist its operations against me, in Jesus' name.

I cancel any and all Rahab assignments against me. I command Rahab's storms to be still. I rebuke Rahab's witchcraft storms now, in Jesus name, and cast all my cares on the Lord. I thank You for the peace of God that passes all understanding to guard my heart and mind against Rahab's retaliation, in Jesus' name.

Endnotes

1. Chuck Pierce, "Chuck Pierce Prophesies 'Dragon' Hovering Over Israel," *Charisma Magazine,* November 25, 2014; https://www.charismamag.com/blogs/prophetic-insight/21895-chuck-pierce-prophesies-dragon-hovering-over-israel; accessed April 20, 2018.

2. Ibid.

Chapter 12

THE DARK

MYSTERY OF MERFOLK SPIRITS

F ROM literature and comic books to video games, and music to film and television—and even professional wrestling and on Starbucks' coffee cups—merfolk are pervasive in pop culture. Merfolk are marine creatures that are part fish and part human—the top half taking on the form of a human and the bottom half taking the form of a fish. These hybrid spirits are seductive, sinister, and elusive and spiritual warriors need to understand their dark mystery.

Merfolk have been in literature and movies since the early 1900s, but P.T. Barnum exhibited what he called the Fiji Mermaid, a skeleton appearing in mermaid form, in 1842. There was Miranda, a seawitch who charmed a doctor into taking her on a journey through London to see the world and seduce men. *The Creature from the Black Lagoon* scared audiences in the 1950s. And the television animated series *Triton* emerged in 1972.

In 1989, Disney's *The Little Mermaid* penetrated pop culture at a high level, introducing our children to the spirit world—and portraying it as much different from what it truly is. The story was based on Hans Christian Andersen's fairy tale by the same name. The book and movie tell the story of a princess mermaid who dreams of becoming a human. Remember, spirits need a human body to work through—either by occupying a place in the soul or by working on the mind to influence the actions and behaviors of their targets.

Benjamin Radford offered some interesting insights in a *LiveScience* article, "Mermaids & Mermen: Facts & Legends." He writes:

> C.J.S. Thompson, a former curator at the Royal College of Surgeons of England, notes in his book *The Mystery and Lore of Monsters* that "Traditions concerning creatures half-human and half-fish in form have existed for thousands of years, and the Babylonian deity Era or Oannes, the Fish-god...is usually depicted as having a bearded head with a crown and a body like a man, but from the waist downwards he has the shape of a fish."

> Greek mythology contains stories of the god Triton, the merman messenger of the sea, and several modern religions including Hinduism and Candomble (an Afro-Brazilian belief) worship mermaid goddesses to this day. In some legends from Scotland and Wales mermaids befriended—and even married—humans. Meri Lao, in her book *Seduction and the Secret Power of Women*, notes that 'In the Shetland Islands, mermaids are stunningly beautiful women who live under the sea; their hybrid appearance is temporary, the effect being achieved by donning the skin of a fish. They must be very careful not to lose this while wandering about on land, because without it they would be unable to return to their underwater realm.[1]

Finding Merfolks Spirits in the Bible

Before we move on, it's important to me that you see the Bible connection here. Although I'm convinced there are many waters spirits who remain unnamed—and that indeed may be described in Greek and Roman mythology—it's vital that we stay biblically grounded in the talk of merfolk spirits. These hybrid spirits are real. We see the merfolk spirit manifest as Dagon in the Bible.

Dagon was the chief God of the Philistines and the father of Baal. The name Dagon means "little fish" and he was known as the storm god, which is often paralleled to a fertility god because storms ruin harvests. According to *Baker's Evangelical Dictionary of Biblical Theology*, it is a diminutive of "dag" which is "a fish, the fish-god; the national god of the Philistines. This idol had the body of a fish with the head and hands of a man. It was an Assyrio-Babylonian deity, the worship of which was introduced among the Philistines through Chaldea. The most famous of the temples of Dagon were at Gaza and Ashdod."

We see Dagon in Judges 16:23-24 in the context of capturing Samson:

> *Now the lords of the Philistines assembled to offer a great sacrifice to Dagon their god, and to rejoice, for they said, "Our god has given Samson our enemy into our hands." When the people saw him, they praised their god, for they said, "Our god has given our enemy into our hands, even the destroyer of our country, who has slain many of us."*

Ellicott's Commentary for English Readers calls Dagon a sea monster—"upward man, downward fish." The commentary reads:

> In 1 Samuel 5:4 we have an allusion to his stump or fish-part. Dag means 'fish,' and the same root is found in Tagus. A goddess

of similar form and attributes was worshipped under the name of Atargatis or Derceto (2 Maccabees 12:26). How widely the worship was spread we see from the commonness of the name Beth-dagon in the Shephelah (Joshua 15:41). His chief temple at Azotus was burned by Judas Maccabeus (1 Maccabees 10:83). The only other Philistine god mentioned in Scripture is Baal-zebub, god of Ekron (2 Kings 1:2-16). [Author's note: The books of 1 and 2 Maccabees are early Jewish writings that are part of the canon of Scripture in the Roman Catholic, Greek and Russian Orthodox and Coptic churches.]

Pulpit Commentary reads:

Dagon (from dag, a fish in Hebrew), the national male god of the Philistines, as Atergatis, or Derceto, was their goddess. Both the male and female divinities seem to have had the head and breast and hands human, and the rest of the body fish-shaped (see 1 Samuel 5:5). The fish was a natural emblem of fertility and productiveness, especially to a maritime people. The fish-shaped idol is found upon old Phoenician coins, and also on the monuments of Khorsabad, and on some Assyrian gems in the British Museum. One of the chief temples of Dagon was at Gaza. Several towns bore the name of Dagon, as Beth-dagon in Judah (Joshua 15:41) and in Asher (Joshua 19:27), Caphar-dagon near Diospolis, etc., showing that the worship of Dagon was widespread.

Dagon's Wicked Agenda Against Believers

As you can see, worship of this God was pervasive and this false god's exaltation dates back further than Baal, who again is the son of Dagon. Dagon is one of the first-ever idols that lost souls worshipped. Today, merfolk—and the idol of Dagon they represent—is idolized by children all around the world through movies and comic books.

Pop star Lady Gaga dressed as a mermaid named Yuyi for one of her music videos. Even Barbie, the famous doll, explores the world of merfolk in direct-to-video movies that are shaping the minds of our children. But this is nothing new. The former generation saw mermaids in *Peter Pan*. Western cultures don't worship Dagon outwardly but celebrate this spirit through media.

Dagon is clearly influencing the hearts and minds of people today and has found a way into the entertainment mountain. In *Buffy the Vampire Slayer*, the "Order of Dagon" protected the Key. The classic *Conan the Barbarian* movies featured Dagon worship, but he was called Dagoth. One gothic underground band named itself after the false god and several other bands sing anthems to this idol. It's no surprise that Dagon is a demon in the roleplaying game Dungeons & Dragons.

Dagon wants to capture your heart so it can capture your anointing. Put another way, Dagon wants your worship so it can displace the presence of God, the Source of your anointing, in your life. Dagon wants to blind you from the truth of who you are and the source of your life. Dagon wants to cut off your authority to pray—he's after your head. You open the door for Dagon—a merfolk spirit—through idolatry. Dagon will bring storms in your life. If you focus on those storms, you will become barren and unfruitful.

Dagon works to capture your heart through idolatry. Any time you worship an idol, you're displacing God from the chief place in your life. What is idolatry? It's when you put something above God in your life. It's when you are more devoted to something than God. That could be a job, a relationship, money, etc. Idolatry is always a danger. The apostle Paul lists it as a work of the flesh (see Galatians 5:20). We'll talk more about idolatry in the next chapter as we learn there how to battle this spirit.

Dagon Works in Spiritual Deception

Like all demons, Dagon works in deception—blinding its victims from the one true and living God. This is what happened to mighty Samson. Samson was holy. He lived under a what we call a Nazarite vow. A Nazarite is someone who takes the vow outlined in Numbers 6:1-21, which essentially speaks of a separation from the things of the world such as wine, growing out the hair, and not going near dead people or other things that defile.

Samson was an enemy to the Philistines and the Philistines were an enemy to Samson. The Philistines, motivated by the false god Dagon, wanted to take down this Nazarite. Samson continued to defy Dagon in a time when Israel was captive to the Philistines. He fell in love with a woman named Delilah. *NOBSE Study Bible Name List* defines Delilah as "lustful." Given Dagon was a god of fertility, this lines up. But Delilah brought a storm into Samson's life.

Here's the backstory: The Philistines bribed Delilah to betray him. Samson's Dagon-inspired enemies promised Delilah a hefty sum to entice him to tell her the source of his strength. At first, Samson wouldn't. But we see the power and persistence of the Delilah Spirit in Judges 16:16, *"It came about when she pressed him daily with her words and urged him, that his soul was annoyed to death."* Strong words. We read the outcome in Judges 16:17-21:

> *So he told her all that was in his heart and said to her, "A razor has never come on my head, for I have been a Nazirite to God from my mother's womb. If I am shaved, then my strength will leave me and I will become weak and be like any other man."*

> *When Delilah saw that he had told her all that was in his heart, she sent and called the lords of the Philistines, saying, "Come up once more, for he has told me all that is in his heart." Then the lords of the Philistines came up to her and brought the money in their hands. She made him sleep on her knees, and*

called for a man and had him shave off the seven locks of his hair. Then she began to afflict him, and his strength left him.

She said, "The Philistines are upon you, Samson!" And he awoke from his sleep and said, "I will go out as at other times and shake myself free." But he did not know that the Lord had departed from him. Then the Philistines seized him and gouged out his eyes; and they brought him down to Gaza and bound him with bronze chains, and he was a grinder in the prison.

While many people attribute the spirit of Delilah for Samson's downfall—and she was the enemy's tool of destruction in his life—we have to remember it was the Dagon Spirit that ultimately influenced Delilah. And it was the Dagon-inspired Philistines who gouged out his eyes. And the Philistines understood this. That's why they had a great sacrifice to Dagon:

Now the lords of the Philistines assembled to offer a great sacrifice to Dagon their god, and to rejoice, for they said, "Our god has given Samson our enemy into our hands." When the people saw him, they praised their god, for they said, 'Our god has given our enemy into our hands, even the destroyer of our country, who has slain many of us (Judges 16:23-24).

Gill's Exposition of the Entire Bible reads:

For they said, our god hath delivered Samson our enemy into our hands; for though Samson's harlot had done it, and they had paid her for it, yet they attribute it to their god, such was their blindness and stupidity; and yet this may shame us believers in the true God, who are so backward to ascribe to him the great things he does for us, when such Heathens were so forward to give glory to their false deities, without any foundation for it.

Dagon Ultimately Wants Your Head

The Spirit of Dagon wants to bring storms in your life to kill, steal, and destroy what God is doing—Dagon wants to kill your spiritual vision, steal your strength, and destroy your dreams. Ultimately, Dagon can't kill so this spirit goes after not just your eyes but your armor and your head.

We find this concept in 1 Chronicles 10 when the Dagon-inspired Philistines fought against Israel. The Philistines killed Jonathan and two of his other sons before their archers wounded the king. Saul ultimately committed suicide so the Philistines would not abuse him. I often wonder if he had Samson in mind, who blindly pushed a grain thresher and was forced to entertain the Philistines before God gave him strength one last time to bring them down.

> It came about the next day, when the Philistines came to strip the slain, that they found Saul and his sons fallen on Mount Gilboa. So they stripped him and took his head and his armor and sent messengers around the land of the Philistines to carry the good news to their idols and to the people. They put his armor in the house of their gods and fastened his head in the house of Dagon (1 Chronicles 10:8-10).

The Philistines cut off his head. Cutting off the head is the ultimate life-extinguishing act. The head represents power, authority, and the center of communication. Dagon attacks your authority—your kingship. Dagon does this through attacking your mind in the midst of the storm, attacks your covenant with a life-giving God, and attacks your identity in Christ.

A Word About Sirens, Nixens, Nymphs, and Ocean Gods

Merfolk spirits are in the category of sirens: hybrid spirits. Isaiah 13:22 (Douay-Rheims Bible) mentions sirens: *"And owls shall answer one another there, in the houses thereof, and sirens in the temples of pleasure."* This verse connects sirens with *"temples of pleasure,"* which gives way to the seductive nature of these spirits.

Sirens, known in some cultures as nixens, have largely become synonymous with mermaids, but they are not mermaids. Noah Webster, who was a Christian, compiled dictionaries. One is called *Webster's Unabridged Dictionary & Bible: New Heart English Bible*. It defines sirens this way:

> One of three sea nymphs—or, according to some writers, of two—said to frequent an island near the coast of Italy, and to sing with such sweetness that they lured mariners to destruction. ...an enticing, dangerous woman; something which is insidious or deceptive; any long, slender amphibian of the genus of Siren or family Sirenidae, destitute of hind legs and pelvis, and having permanent external gills as well as lungs. They inhabit the swamps, lagoons, and ditches of the Southern United States.[2]

While a mermaid is half fish and half human, a siren is half bird, half human, according to Greek mythology,[3] and were children of the river gods. Typically, they played any number of musical instruments but often harps and as the art world evolved male sirens gave way to female sirens as a deadly seductresses. Speaking of the siren, the great artist Leonardo da Vinci wrote, "The siren sings so sweetly that she lulls the mariners to sleep; then she climbs upon the ships and kills the sleeping mariners."

In Scottish mythology we find ashrays, which are known as water lovers but often viewed as sea ghosts, and the "blue men of minch" supposedly lived in caves under the water and emerged to wreck ships passing by. Australian mythology points to Bunyip, which means devil. These creatures reportedly hang out in riverbeds, waterholes, and swamps and cry out at night. They are blamed for crop failures and disease outbreaks. Grindyblows are mentioned in British folklore that drown children. Camaroon folklore speaks of Jengu, which look like mermen that serve as mediums between the living and the dead.

Greek and Roman mythology have no lack of ocean gods. I don't believe each are tied to a spirit but many of them are hybrid creatures, like the Nereides, which are the daughter of sea nymphs that promised sailors and fishermen protection; Nereus, who was known as a shapeshifter with a prophetic voice sporting a male upper body and a fish tail instead of legs. Then there's Oceanus, which had horns like bulls, a male torso, and a serpentine tail. Palaimon was drawn as a child with a fish tail who often rode a dolphin. Phorkys was another fish-tailed god of the sea with craw claws carrying a torch. Skylla appears much like a mermaid but with a warring persona. This is short list of the water spirits of the world, in addition to the ones mentioned earlier in the book.

Remember this, Dagon or any other spirit cannot deceive you until it first seduces you. Remember, Delilah deceived Samson in the context of seduction. Sirens and merman spirits work in the realm of seduction—tapping into the idolatry in your heart as bait to capture you and draw you into its temple. We'll talk about how to overcome this spirit in the next chapter.

Endnotes

1. Benjamin Radford, "Mermaids & Mermen: Facts & Legends," *LIVE-SCIENCE,* May 25, 2017; https://www.livescience.com/39882-mermaid.html; accessed April 21, 2018.

2. https://books.google.com/books?id=Cd5HDwAAQBA-J&pg=PT12746&lpg=PT12746&dq=siren+in+the+bible&source=bl&ots=voQuv4jsT3&sig=qXyCarhFbTjG-Lhs7bhG-BoufWAg&hl=en&sa=X&ved=0ahUKEwjR2uH8xpHZAhWFp-FkKHaMnDb04FBDoAQguMAE#v=onepage&q=siren%20in%20the%20bible&f=false; accessed April 21, 2018.

3. https://en.wikipedia.org/wiki/Siren_(mythology); accessed April 21, 2018.

Chapter 13

OVERCOMING
THE INFLUENCE OF MERMAN SPIRITS

B Y now, you have probably had an entirely new perspective on Starbucks' cups, fairy tales about mermaids and Triton action figures that ultimately celebrate the spirit of Dagon.

Although we don't need to fear drinking out of a cup depicting a mermaid or a toy on a shelf in Walmart—and although we don't need to fear merman spirits—we should be aware of how pervasive this idol is in societies all around the world. Awareness is the first step toward deliverance and ultimate victory.

In the last chapter, we discussed the agenda of the merman—or Dagon—spirit. In summary, Dagon wants to capture your heart so it can capture your anointing. Dagon wants your worship so it can displace the presence of God, the Source of your anointing in your life. Dagon wants to blind you from the truth of who you are and the Source of your life. Dagon wants to cut off your authority to pray—he's after your head.

The good news is you can overcome Dagon attacks against your life. The Kingdom of God is unshakable—but Dagon is not. Dagon can be displaced in your life. This false god falls and must bow in the name of Jesus. Indeed, the Holy Spirit, who inspired all Scripture, left us an account of the demise of Dagon that we'll dive into in a moment.

The Demise of Dagon

We find the victory account in 1 Samuel 5, which is in the context of Samson's apparent defeat discussed in the previous chapter. First Samuel 5:1-2 reads: *"Now the Philistines took the ark of God and brought it from Ebenezer to Ashdod. Then the Philistines took the ark of God and brought it to the house of Dagon and set it by Dagon."*

Let's stop right there and break this down in the context of defeating Dagon. Even if you end up in the house of Dagon—even if you walk into a place where Dagon has a stronghold—the God inside you is bigger than the god that's influencing the atmosphere around you. First John 4:4 assures us, *"Greater is He who is in you than he who is in the world."* Your God is stronger than Dagon. Dagon is in the world. While you find yourself in the world, you are not of the world (see John 17:16). This world is not your home (see Hebrews 13:14). You are a citizen of heaven and have authority over Dagon (see Philippians 3:20).

First Samuel 5:3 goes on to say, *"When the Ashdodites arose early the next morning, behold, Dagon had fallen on his face to the ground before the ark of the Lord...."* Every demon power, including Dagon, must fall at the name of Jesus. Philippians 2:9-11 guarantees this reality as God bestowed on Jesus, *"...the name which is above every name, so that at the name of Jesus every knee will bow, of those who are in heaven and on earth and under the earth, and that every tongue will confess that Jesus Christ is Lord, to the glory of God the Father."*

Like any spiritual battle, saying the name of Jesus one time doesn't always produce immediate results. This is illustrated in the unseen battle against Dagon in the second half of 1 Samuel 5:3: *"So they took Dagon and set him in his place again."*

Dagon is not easily displaced because this ancient spirit has many entry-ways into the minds and hearts of people and, as a principality, can influence regions. In ancient days, Dagon influenced chief cities of the Euphrates around the Balikh and Khabur rivers, according to the Jewish Virtual Library.[1] These were known as "the lands of Dagon." Today, this is the Middle East. But Dagon is not relegated to this region. This marine demon works to establish strongholds in areas with significant rivers.

God always defeats Dagon, as we see in 1 Samuel 5:4, *"But when they arose early the next morning, behold, Dagon had fallen on his face to the ground before the ark of the Lord. And the head of Dagon and both the palms of his hands were cut off on the threshold; only the trunk of Dagon was left to him."*

Ellicott's Commentary for English Readers expounds:

> No mere accident could account for what had happened. The head and hands were severed from the image, and thrown contemptuously on the threshold of the temple, upon which the foot of every priest or worshipper as he passed into the sacred house must tread.... The Hebrew, rendered literally, would run, only Dagon was left to him: that is to say, only "the fish," the least noble part of the idol image, was left standing; the human head and hands were tossed down for men as they passed in to trample on; "only the form of a fish was left in him."

I find *Benson's Commentary* on this insightful and empowering: "The head is the seat of wisdom; the hands the instruments of action; both are cut off, to show that he had neither wisdom nor strength to defend himself or his worshippers." This is similar to Queen Jezebel's fate after the eunuchs threw her down at Jehu's command: *"They went to bury her, but they found nothing more of her than the skull and the feet and the palms of her hands"* (2 Kings 9:35).

Worshipping God Overwhelms Dagon

God Himself took out Dagon. It was God's presence that overpowered this marine demon sitting on its pedestal. If you want to defeat Dagon's influence in your life or city, cultivating an atmosphere thick with God's presence is a key strategy. This makes spiritual and natural sense. With idolatry, you're giving praise, worship, and adoration to a god other than Jehovah. And we know God inhabits the praises of His people (see Psalm 22:3). We empower what we exalt. When we exalt God and Him alone through praise, worship, adoration, thanksgiving, and the like, we will displace idols.

Praise and worship as a prophetic warfare strategy is never wrong, but with Dagon it is especially effective given this tactic is outlined in the Bible. In Joshua 6, praise brought down the walls at Jericho. David's anointed worship sent devils fleeing from Saul (see 1 Samuel 16:14-17, 23). Psalm 32:7 speaks of songs of deliverance.

David put it this way in Psalm 34:1-7 (NKJV):

> *I will bless the Lord at all times; His praise will continually be in my mouth. My soul will make its boast in the Lord; the humble will hear of it and be glad. Oh, magnify the Lord with me, and let us exalt His name together. I sought the Lord, and He answered me, and delivered me from all my fears. They looked to Him and became radiant, and their faces are not ashamed. This poor man cried, and the Lord heard, and saved him out of all his troubles. The angel of the Lord camps around those who fear Him, and delivers them.*

Get into the psalms as you worship. Declare Scriptures like Psalm 29:2 and make it personal: *"Ascribe to the Lord the glory due to His name; worship the Lord in holy array."* Even if your voice crackles and even through tears, sing Psalm 95:1-6:

O come, let us sing for joy to the Lord, let us shout joyfully to the rock of our salvation. Let us come before His presence with thanksgiving, let us shout joyfully to Him with psalms. For the Lord is a great God and a great King above all gods, in whose hand are the depths of the earth, the peaks of the mountains are His also. The sea is His, for it was He who made it, and His hands formed the dry land. Come, let us worship and bow down, let us kneel before the Lord our Maker.

When the song of sirens—the song of seducing temptation—is blaring in your ears, tune it out by praising and worshipping the Lord! Get out of Dagon's temple. Be like David, who declared in Psalm 27:4-6:

One thing I have asked from the Lord, that I shall seek: That I may dwell in the house of the Lord all the days of my life, to behold the beauty of the Lord and to meditate in His temple. For in the day of trouble He will conceal me in His tabernacle; in the secret place of His tent He will hide me; He will lift me up on a rock. And now my head will be lifted up above my enemies around me, and I will offer in His tent sacrifices with shouts of joy; I will sing, yes, I will sing praises to the Lord.

Flee Idolatry Immediately

Inspired by the Holy Spirit, Paul told us to flee from idolatry (see 1 Corinthians 10:14). The Word of God never instructs us to do something the grace of God won't empower us to do if we simply get into agreement. Of course, you can't flee something you don't see. Take some time now to pray and ask the Lord if you have idolatry in your heart.

Deception is progressive. It starts with those little foxes. Guarding our hearts from deception means being humble enough to acknowledge that we are capable of being deceived—of falling into idolatry. It also means setting our minds on Christ and putting first the Kingdom. As far as the world is concerned we have died, and our real life is hidden with Christ in God (Colossians 3:3). Guarding ourselves from deception, then, means taking the apostle Paul's advice:

> *Kill (deaden, deprive of power) the evil desire lurking in your members [those animal impulses and all that is earthly in you that is employed in sin]: sexual vice, impurity, sensual appetites, unholy desires, and all greed and covetousness, for that is idolatry (the deifying of self and other created things instead of God)* (Colossians 3:5 AMPC).

Keep in mind we can't blame all this deception business on the devil. Nor can we be ignorant of his devices. Part of his ministry is to find the idolatry in our hearts: the deceitfulness of riches, the pride of life, the lust of the flesh, or something else that causes us to give God's place to another. Once satan finds that idolatry, he'll tempt you with it. At that point we have a clear choice: destroy the idol or walk into darkness.

Take some time now to examine yourself. Idolatry is usually rooted in one of three areas. John the apostle pointed them out in 1 John 2:16 (AMPC):

> *For all that is in the world—the lust of the flesh [craving for sensual gratification] and the lust of the eyes [greedy longings of the mind] and the pride of life [assurance in one's own resources or in the stability of earthly things]—these do not come from the Father but are from the world [itself].*

Find the idolatry in your heart before the devil does. If the enemy has already lured you into temptation through idolatry, repent. Ask the Lord to forgive you and strengthen you.

Cutting Off Dagon's Head

Once you've rooted idolatry out of your life, it's easy to cut off Dagon's head with praise and worship. Radical warriors don't just plow over the fruit of a demonic attack—such as oppression or sickness—they cut off the head of the attack. David understood it wasn't enough to slay the giant attacking him as he made intercession for Israel. He knew he had to cut off Goliath's head.

Especially noteworthy is the reality that Goliath was a Philistine and under the influence of Dagon. First Samuel 17:43 tells us, *"the Philistine cursed David by his gods."* Dagon was the chief god of the Philistines. I can only imagine the righteous indignation in David's heart hearing Goliath release curses by these false idols. Let's look at the rest of the account of this prophetic showdown between a God-lover and a Dagon-lover.

> *The Philistine also said to David, "Come to me, and I will give your flesh to the birds of the sky and the beasts of the field." Then David said to the Philistine, "You come to me with a sword, a spear, and a javelin, but I come to you in the name of the Lord of hosts, the God of the armies of Israel, whom you have taunted. This day the Lord will deliver you up into my hands, and I will strike you down and remove your head from you. And I will give the dead bodies of the army of the Philistines this day to the birds of the sky and the wild beasts of the earth, that all the earth may know that there is a God in Israel, and that all this assembly may know that the Lord does not deliver by sword or by spear; for the battle is the Lord's and He will give you into our hands" (1 Samuel 17:44-47).*

David didn't fear Goliath or the Dagon he served—and neither should you. The Bible tells us David ran to the battle line. He didn't walk. He didn't inch his way forward in fear. He didn't take one step forward and two steps back. He ran to the battle line with a passion for his God and a confidence in his heart that Jehovah Nissi was his victory banner.

> *Thus David prevailed over the Philistine with a sling and a stone, and he struck the Philistine and killed him; but there was no sword in David's hand. Then David ran and stood over the Philistine and took his sword and drew it out of its sheath and killed him, and cut off his head with it. When the Philistines saw that their champion was dead, they fled* (1 Samuel 17:50-51).

You have to cut off the head of your attacker! Biblically speaking, the head represents power, authority, and the center of communication. When the enemy rears his ugly head, you need to cut it off! Cut off the power he has over you—power you gave him through ignorance or idolatry. Cut off the authority you've given him by coming into agreement with his lies. Cut off his words—the vain imaginations that you allowed a higher place in your soul than the Word of God. Cut off the enemy's head with the Sword of the Spirit, which is the Word of God (see Ephesians 6:17).

A Brief Word About Baal

Where you find Dagon, you'll also find Baal, his son. In many ways, this is a spiritual parallel to the saying, "Like father, like son." Baal leads people into idolatry just like it led the Israelites into idolatry when Moses was up on the mountain talking with God.

Remember when the children of Israel made a molten calf as an idol to worship? That was the spirit of Baal (see Exodus 32:8). Baal is a god of prophetic divination. Baal is the god of rain, thunder, fertility, and agriculture. Canaanite mythology tells us Baal was the son of the chief god El and the goddess of the sea, Asherah. These were the gods Queen Jezebel worshipped. Baal's "sisters" are Ashtoreth, a fertility goddess, and the goddess of war Anath.

Baal is a principality in the Ephesians 6 hierarchy often illustrated in mythology as holding a lightning bolt in his hand and, like Jezebel, is associated with perversion. Jesus called Beelzebub, another name for Baal, the ruler of demons, in Matthew 12:24 (NKJV). He is known as the god of 1,000 faces because he influences many other "gods" and spirits, such as Marduk, Osiris, Prometheus, Jupiter, and Bacchus.

Baal releases witchcraft and works closely with the spirits of Jezebel and Leviathan, as well as various other occult-related demons. Where you find Baal, you'll find sexual perversion, especially homosexuality. There are variations of the name of Baal, including Baal-hamon, which means "the lord of wealth or abundance" and Baal-berith, which means "the lord of the covenant." Remember, it was the Baal spirit that wooed Israel into spiritual adultery and bondage throughout its history.

When battling Dagon, look out for Baal. Like Dagon, you can't beat Baal without repentance. If you have common ground with Baal—if you are chasing power and wealth or are ensnared by sexual perversion—you must repent. As with any principality, defeating a spirit like Dagon or Baal demands corporate unity. But you must first strip these demons of any right they have through your agreement in thought, word, or deed before you can exercise your authority over them, in Jesus' name.

A Daring Prayer Against Dagon

Father, in the name of Jesus, I come into Your presence casting down my idols. I will have no other God before You. I abolish every idol in my life and commit to serving You and You alone. Forgive me for allowing anything to stand between us and help me to keep my eyes and heart focused on You and only You, because You are worthy of all my praise.

I break the assignment of Dagon to capture my heart and defile my spirit. I stand against Dagon's attempts to hinder the flow of Your anointing through me to minister Your Gospel. I push back Dagon's darkness in my life with wholehearted worship. Lord, help me worship You in spirit and in truth. Remove anything from my heart that hinders love, in Jesus' name.

I obliterate Dagon's daring plans to blind me from the truth. Open the eyes of my heart, Lord, so that I can see You as You really are and see the enemy of my soul as he really is. Lord, give me a revelation of the truth that sets me free from every Dagon and Baal attack. I stand in my authority and demolish Dagon's head now, in Jesus name.

Endnote

1. Jewish Virtual Library, "Encyclopedia Judaica: Dagon"; http://www. jewishvirtuallibrary.org/dagon; accessed April 21, 2018.

Chapter 14

BEWARE

BEHEMOTH: THE SPIRIT
THAT CROSSES LAND AND SEA

WHILE unclean spirits hate the water (see Matthew 12:43) and some spirits operate solely in the waters, there is a principality worth noting that crosses both realms. Also called a hippopotamus in the Bible, a Behemoth Spirit crosses land and sea and builds systems that oppress people across two of the three strongholds in creation. These are widespread strongholds, like Communism or Islam, which affect the masses.

God speaks about Behemoth in Job 40:15-24:

> *Behold now, Behemoth, which I made as well as you; he eats grass like an ox. Behold now, his strength in his loins and his power in the muscles of his belly. He bends his tail like a cedar; the sinews of his thighs are knit together. His bones are tubes of bronze; his limbs are like bars of iron.*

He is the first of the ways of God; let his maker bring near his sword. Surely the mountains bring him food, and all the beasts of the field play there. Under the lotus plants he lies down, in the covert of the reeds and the marsh. The lotus plants cover him with shade; the willows of the brook surround him. If a river rages, he is not alarmed; he is confident, though the Jordan rushes to his mouth. Can anyone capture him when he is on watch, with barbs can anyone pierce his nose?

The Mystery of Behemoth

Behemoth is not your garden variety demon—it's a monstrous principality. Paul lists principalities in his hierarchy of demons in Ephesians 6:12. The Behemoth Spirit has not gained rock star demon status like Jezebel or Baal. But make no mistake, this spirit that crosses land and sea is active in the nations. Let's start our study with what the Bible says about Behemoth.

The KJV Old Testament Hebrew Lexicon defines behemoth this way: "perhaps an extinct dinosaur; a Diplodocus or Brachiosaurus, exact meaning unknown. Some translate as an elephant or a hippopotamus, but from the description in Job 40:15-24, this is patently absurd."

And that's where the debate begins and may be why much of the church has neglected the warfare this spirit brings. Behemoth is a bit of a mystery, indeed, which is part of why it's so effective.

The Body of Christ is largely ignorant of its devices. Some claim there is no Behemoth Spirit. Others claim it's just a system. Still others say it may be a dinosaur. Some says it's an elephant, rhinoceros, hippopotamus, river horse, sea horse, sea ox, or water ox. Keep in mind as you read these commentaries that the physical descriptions inform the spiritual characteristics or attack modes of this spirit.

Treasury of Scripture offers an entirely different take:

> Behemoth or, the elephant, as some think...the hippopot-
> amus, or river horse. It is nearly as large as the elephant;
> its head is enormously large, its mouth very wide, the jaws
> extending upwards of two feet, armed with four cutting
> teeth, each twelve inches long; its hide is so tough and so
> thick as to resist the strokes of a sabre, and it thinly cov-
> ered with hair of lightish colour; its legs are three feet long;
> though amphibious, its hoofs, which are quadrified??, are
> unconnected; and its tail is naked, about a foot in length,
> but exceedingly thick and strong. It inhabits the rivers of
> Africa; feeds on grass and other vegetables; moves slowly
> and heavily; swims dexterously; sleeps in reedy places; has
> a tremendous voice between the lowing of the ox and the
> roar of the elephant; and when irritated, will attack boats
> and men with fury.)

Consider for a moment the strength of the hippo when considering the power of this spirit. Hippos are especially awkward and ugly creatures but they are graceful in water and strong swimmers that can hold their breath for up to five minutes, according to *National Geographic.*[1] Their eyes and noses are high on their heads so they can remain almost completely submerged and still see above the water. Hippos are the third-largest living mammals. Only the elephant and white rhino are larger, according to *LiveScience.*[2] They can grow up to nearly 17 feet and weigh up to 10,000 pounds. That is certainly a behemoth!

"Hippos are very aggressive creatures and are very dangerous," *LiveScience* reports. "They have large teeth and tusks that they use for fighting off others that they see as threats, including humans. Sometimes, their young are the victims of their temper. During a fight between two adults, a young hippo can be hurt or crushed."

Gill's Exposition of the Entire Bible suggests:

> Behold, now behemoth.... The word is plural, and signifies beasts, and may be used to denote the chiefest and largest of beasts...that a land animal should eat grass is not so wonderful; but that a creature who lives in the water should come out of it and eat grass is very strange and worthy of admiration, it is observed: and that the river horse feeds in corn fields and on grass many writers assure us; yea, in the river it feeds not on fishes, but on the roots of the water lily, which fishermen therefore use to bait their hooks with to take it. Nor is it unlike an ox in its shape, and in some parts of its body: hence the Italians call it "bomaris," the "sea ox"; but it is double the size of an ox. Olaus Magnus speaks of a sea horse, found between Britain and Norway; which has the head of a horse, and neighs like one; has cloven feet with hoofs like a cow; and seeks its food both in the sea and on the land, and grows to the bigness of an ox, and has a forked tail like a fish.

Behemoth's Cunning Characteristics

The Bible itself outlines some of Behemoth's physical characteristics. First, we see his strength is in his loins (see Job 40:16). The loins speak of the reproductive area. One of Behemoth's strengths is its ability to reproduce its agenda, which is how it has created systemic strongholds in the earth—belief systems that blind people to God or keep them in bondage.

Job 40:16 also speaks to his power in the muscles of his belly. The Hebrew word for "belly" in this verse is *beten*. According to *The KJV Old Testament Hebrew Lexicon*, it means, "belly, womb, body." But drilling down into the definitions offers a deeper meaning: "seat of hunger; seat of mental faculties;

depth of Sheol (fig.)." Here again we see the concept of a womb—which conceives and gives birth. But we also see Behemoth is hungry and has a mind set on hell. Behemoth works to bring hell's agenda to earth, birthing nefarious antichrist ideologies.

Job 40:17 tells us Behemoth moves his tail like a cedar. This is especially telling of its power. A cedar tree is an object of admiration in the Bible. Isaiah 35:2 says the cedar is the *"glory of Lebanon"* and its height higher than any other trees with many branches (see Ezekiel 31:5). Behemoth rises high on the demonic ranking as a principality to cross over and into the seven mountains of societal influence. In other words, Behemoth's reach is widespread. Like the US government has branches—legislative, executive, and judicial— Behemoth has many branches or divisions.

In the Bible, cedars are often celebrated plant life. Cedars are considered majestic (see 2 Kings 14:9) and excellent (see Song of Solomon 5:15). Cedars have an aromatic smell. *ATS Bible Dictionary* explains, "The gum, which exudes both from the trunk and the cones or fruits, is soft like balsam of Mecca." Everything about this tree has a strong balsamic odor; and hence the whole grove is so pleasant and fragrant, that it is delightful to walk in it. But there is a dark side. Although it has an aromatic smell, this seduction is deceptive. *Smith's Bible Dictionary* points out the cedar has a bitter taste. Behemoth woos people with its aromatic odor but offers a bitter bite. This spirit plays off bitterness in the hearts and minds of people to inject its hostile ideologies into human souls.

According to *ATS Bible Dictionary*, "The wood is peculiarly adapted to building, because it is not subject to decay, nor to be eaten of worms; hence it was much used for rafters, and for boards with which to cover houses and form the floors and ceilings of rooms. It was of a red color, beautiful, solid, and free from knots. The palace of Persepolis, the temple at Jerusalem, and Solomon's palace, were all in this way built with cedar...." The structures Behemoth builds are attractive to both intellectuals and those who would rather not think for themselves—and once the structure is built, it's difficult to tear down.

Also in Job 40:17 we see *"the sinews of his thighs are knit together."* *Merriam-Webster* defines sinew as "solid resilient strength" and "the chief supporting force." Behemoth is a resilient spirit; not one to give up easily in its hellish work. As for Behemoth's bones, Job 20:18 calls them *"tubes of bronze."*

When you find bronze, brass, or copper heavens—when it feels like a hard heaven and your payers don't seem to be working—you'll often find Behemoth's systems are prevailing. Bronze heavens are part of the curse of the law (see Deuteronomy 28:23). Bronze is a mixture of metals—not pure like gold or silver. According to *Sciencing.com,* "It is extremely strong and resistant to atmospheric corrosion. It has been used since prehistoric times to forge tools, weapons, statues and ornaments."[3]

Where Behemoth rules, you'll find strong resistance to the Gospel. You'll find it hard to displace from the atmosphere as it is resilient and resistant to atmospheric corrosion. That's why you feel your prayers are going up and falling flat.

Job 40:18 also shares Behemoth's limbs are like bars of iron. This again speaks to the strength of this spirit. The Hebrew word for iron in this verse is *barzel,* which means harshness, strength and, figuratively speaking, oppression. Behemoth is indeed a harsh spirit that brings its strength to bare on a mind or region to create a climate of oppression. Iron is an element of steel and its strongly magnetic, according to *The Balance.com.*[4] The Behemoth Spirit works like a magnet on the mind, pulling you into its false belief systems and structures.

Behemoth can be found under the lotus plants and in the covert of the reeds and the marsh (Job 40:22). The King James says "shady trees." The Hebrew word for "covert" in this verse is *cether.* *The KJV Old Testament Hebrew Lexicon* defines it as "covering, shelter, hiding place, secrecy, secret place and secrecy (of tongue being slanderous)." This reveals Behemoth lies in hidden places and works in secrecy—and works, in part, in the realm of slander. Slander is to make a false spoken statement that causes people to have a bad opinion of someone, according to *Merriam-Webster*. It means to defame, malign, vilify, and asperse, which is a fancy word for a continued attack on someone's reputation.

Job 40:23 gives us more insight into Behemoth's boldness. The Bible says he's not alarmed if the river rages. The word for "alarmed" in that verse is the Hebrew word *chaphaz*. The lexicon tells us it means "to hurry, flee, hasten, fear, be terrified." Behemoth doesn't tremble if a storm comes against it—the King James translation says he trusts he can draw up Jordan in his mouth. Again, we see Behemoth depends much on his mouth as his strength—and indeed part of his strength is in his mouth.

The Voice of Behemoth

How does Behemoth attack? What does its voice sound like? *Treasury Scripture* mentions Behemoth's "mouth is very wide, the jaws extending upwards of two feet, armed with cutting teeth, each twelve inches long." Spiritually speaking, Behemoth has a loud voice that amplifies beyond the personal level to societies and even nations. His words are cutting and biting.

Gill's Exposition of the Entire Bible suggests Behemoth neighs like a horse. A neigh is a prolonged cry, according to *Merriam-Webster. Dictionary.com* offers the definition whinny. This falls in the realm of yelling. Yelling is to "cry out or speak with a strong, loud, clear shout." *LiveScience* reports: "Hippos are very loud animals. Their snorts, grumbles and wheezes have been measured at 115 decibels, according to the San Diego Zoo—about the same volume as being 15 feet (4.6 m) from the speakers at a rock concert. Hippos also use subsonic vocalizations to communicate."

Behemoth is a voice that will be heard strong, loud, and clear as it shouts lies at your mind and into cities, nations, governments and world systems. Make no mistake, Behemoth is influencing the seven mountains of culture—name them. Entire books have been written on the seven mountains of society. Beyond Bright and Cunningham, men of God like Francis Schaeffer, Bob Buford, Os Hillman, Ed Silvoso, and Lance Wallnau have worked to forward this revelation. Every believer has been given a sphere of influence and authority in one of these mountains: religion, family, arts and entertainment, business, education, government, and media.

What is Behemoth saying? Behemoth speaks lies that blind people to the truth of God's Word. We gain some knowledge into how a Behemoth operates at this level through a standard dictionary definition. *Merriam-Webster* defines behemoth as "something of monstrous size, power, or appearance." *Dictionary.com* tells us it's "any creature or thing of monstrous size or power."

John Eckhardt defines behemoth as "any system large enough in size or power to oppress multitudes of people. It can be a religious, political, cultural or economic system—and even a blend of those, as in the case with communism. Behemoths are erected by the enemy to keep the Gospel out and multitudes of people in darkness." He goes on to say, "Behemoths are strongholds that must be broken in order to see millions of people released from darkness and come into the glorious light of the knowledge of Jesus Christ. Yet these demonic 'giants' have been around for generations."[5]

In her book *Rules of Engagement: The Art of Strategic Prayer and Spiritual Warfare*, Cindy Trimm defines Behemoth as "an oppressive, powerful hippopotamus-like creature, known for its supernatural strength. It affects ideologies, political/military strength, and religious/cultural strongholds; involves witchcraft (control); may take years to dismantle/destroy (communication); and becomes violent when attacked."

Behemoths manifest as false religions and ideologies. That's a broad spectrum, given any religion or ideology that does not align with the Word of God is false. Let's look at some Behemoths in each of the seven mountains.

The Religion Mountain

In the religion mountain, false gospels are Behemoths. Behemoth works with another principality called antichrist to propagate false religious structures. I won't name every religion one by one, but the rapid rise of gospels that do not name Jesus as Lord is part of Behemoth's structure. False religions are dangerous because they send people to hell, and many false religions also leave people living in a hell on earth, punishing themselves, sacrificing their bodies in terror attacks, or leaving them living in constant guilt or trying to earn their way to heaven.

The Family Mountain

In the family mountain, divorce is a Behemoth. Most marriages in the United States don't make it twenty years, according to the National Survey of Family Growth. Malachi 2:16 tells us God hates divorce. Why does God hate divorce? Divorce damages the soul. It causes hurts, wounds, the pain of separation. Divorce causes feelings of failure and loneliness. That's not to mention the damage it does to the children of divorced parents.

The Arts and Entertainment Mountain

In the arts and entertainment mountain, perversion is a Behemoth. Hollywood scandals have erupted demonstrating widespread child abuse and sexual harassment. Hollywood propagates graphic violence, sexual immorality, perversion, foul language, and ideology that molds the minds of young children, youth, and even adults to defy the Word of God.

The Business Mountain

In the business mountain, Babylon is a Behemoth. The love of money is a root of all evil (see 1 Timothy 6:10), but money is itself is not evil. God has given us the power to create wealth to establish His covenant on the earth (see Deuteronomy 8:18). But Behemoth works with greed and a Babylonian Spirit.

A Babylonian Spirit drives people to build and make a name for themselves instead of bringing glory to God (see Genesis 11). The Babylonian Spirit spurs idolatry in the hearts of people. We know covetousness is idolatry (see Colossians 3:5). Revelation 18:4 says, *"I heard another voice from heaven, saying, "Come out of her, my people, so that you will not participate in her sins and receive of her plagues."* We know that the Behemoth of Babylon is going to fall in a day (see Revelation 18:1-3).

The Education Mountain

In the education mountain, humanism is a Behemoth. *Merriam-Webster* defines humanism as "a doctrine, attitude or way of life centered on human interests or values; especially: a philosophy that usually rejects supernaturalism and stresses an individual's dignity and worth and capacity for self-realization through reason." As Cindy Jacobs points out in her book *The Reformation Manifesto,* "Humanism has become manifested through progressivism and naturalistic theory, which omit any reference to God or religion. By the 1960s, these ideologies controlled the power bases of education at all levels. In other words, they transformed society through education."[6]

The Government Mountain

In the government mountain, we've seen several Behemoths rise. These include Marxism, communism, and fascism. Let's look at the *Merriam-Webster* definitions of each. Marxism is "the political, economic, and social principles and policies advocated by Marx; especially: a theory and practice of socialism...including the labor theory of value, dialectical materialism, the class struggle, and dictatorship of the proletariat until the establishment of a classless society."

Communism is "a system in which goods are owned in common and are available to all as needed: a theory advocating elimination of private property;" "a totalitarian system of government in which a single authoritarian party controls state-owned means of production."

Fascism is "a political philosophy, movement, or regime (such as that of the Fascisti) that exalts nation and often race above the individual and that stands for a centralized autocratic government headed by a dictatorial leader, severe economic and social regimentation, and forcible suppression of opposition." Keep in mind, Adolph Hitler, who was responsible for the murder of over six million Jews, was a fascist, as was Italy's Benito Mussolini.

The Media Mountain

In the media mountain, propaganda is Behemoth. *Merriam-Webster* defines propaganda as "the spreading of ideas, information, or rumor for the purpose of helping or injuring an institution, cause, or a person;" "ideas, facts or allegations spread deliberately to further one's cause or to damage an opposing cause." Rulers on other mountains use the media to forward its agenda. The media mountain is essential to satan's strategy to advance his agenda on the other mountains of influence.

As you can see, Behemoths are nothing to play with—but they can be torn down incrementally. They can fall down in a day when we use God's Word like a hammer. Behemoth's ideologies can crumble like the Berlin wall. One day, they will all fall and their adherents will bow to the name of Jesus. Until then, we must guard ourselves from Behemoth's influence and be led to take on the battles—and only the battles—with Behemoth that He calls us to fight. We'll explore this more in the next chapter.

Endnotes

1. *National Geographic,* "Hippopotamus"; https://www.nationalgeographic. com/animals/mammals/h/hippopotamus/; accessed April 21, 2018.

2. Alina Bradford, "Hippo Facts"; *LiveScience,* October 30, 2014; https:// www.livescience.com/27339-hippos.html; accessed April 21, 2018.

3. Bert Markgraf, "The Characteristics of Bronze Metals"; *Sciencing,* April 25, 2017; https://sciencing.com/characteristics-bronze-met- als-8162597.html; accessed April 21, 2018.

4. Terence Bell, "Metal Profile: Iron"; *TheBalance,* April 2, 2018; https:// www.thebalance.com/metal-profile-iron-2340139; accessed April 21, 2018.

5. John Eckhardt, *Behemoth and Leviathan* (Crusaders Ministries, 1994).

6. Cindy Jacobs, *The Reformation Manifesto* (Bloomington, MN: Bethany House Publishers, 2009), 116.

Chapter 15

BATTLING
BEHEMOTH STRONGHOLDS

B EHEMOTH is cunning. His mouth is wide. His teeth are cutting—but this principality is not invincible. You can battle Behemoth's strongholds in your life and in your city—in Christ.

Battling Behemoth is not for the faint of heart and it's not a short-term skirmish.

Jamieson-Fausset-Brown Bible Commentary suggests in this passage, "God shows that if Job cannot bring under control the lower animals (of which he selects the two most striking, behemoth on land, leviathan in the water), much less is he capable of governing the world."

However, James 3:7 tells us, *"Every species of beasts and birds, of reptiles and creatures of the sea, is tamed and has been tamed by the human race."* God gave us dominion over the beasts of the field and the fish of the sea and assures us we can trample on serpents and scorpions and nothing shall by any means harm us (see Luke 10:19).

Apart from Christ, we're no match for Behemoth in any of its manifestations. But with the Lord on our side, we can push back the darkness Behemoth brings into our minds and over our societies. It takes time—we have to break free in our hearts and minds first—but Behemoths can be torn down with the voice of the Lord, which is like a hammer. Psalm 29:4-5 tells us, *"the voice of Yahweh breaks the cedars"*—and Behemoth is compared to cedar.

Behemoth's Insidious Ideologies

Behemoth works through insidious ideologies. It's important to understand the definition of ideology in the context of this principality the Bible calls Behemoth. *Merriam-Webster* defines ideology as "a systematic body of concepts especially about human life or culture; a manner or the content of thinking characteristic of an individual, group, or culture; and the integrated assertions, theories and aims that constitute a sociopolitical program." *Dictionary.com* adds "the body of doctrine, myth, belief, etc., that guides an individual, social movement, institution, class, or large group."

The Lord spoke to me in 2017 about a movement of movements. We've seen prayer movements rising, house church movements rising, apostolic and prophetic movements rising, and more. But not all rising movements are good—or originating from the heart God. We're seeing feminism movements and neo-Nazi movements rising even while deep-rooted Behemoths like racism, communism, evolution, and false religions continue to remain entrenched in various cultures and societies.

Mark Twain once said, "It ain't what you don't know that gets you into trouble. It's what you know for sure that just ain't so." Behemoth works through spreading false ideologies that become strongholds in minds, cultures, societies, and even whole nations. Behemoths use the media as a weapon of disinformation dissemination. Media is one of the main propagators of false ideology and demonic propaganda.

Propaganda is "spreading of ideas, information, or rumor for the purpose of helping or injuring an institution, a cause, or a person" and "ideas, facts, or allegations spread deliberately to further one's cause or to damage an opposing cause; also : a public action having such an effect," according to *Merriam-Webster.* Word War II saw Nazi propaganda that spread an ideology of murder. Communist propaganda in the former Soviet Union influenced public opinion with messages like, "All power to the Soviets. Peace to the People. Land to the peasants." However, studies show communism always produces poverty. Meanwhile, cult propaganda spreads false religions with promises of peace or power but bring discord and deception.

Make no mistake—even if a news channel claims it's fair and balanced, it has a bias. Advertising entices. Talk shows seek to sway public opinion. Reality television isn't real. Social media is a stomping ground for various agendas. Everyone has an agenda—even Christians. Our agenda is to see people saved, healed, delivered, and equipped. But any agenda—any ideology—beyond the agenda of the Lamb of God and His Holy Spirit according to the Father's will is skewed and mass media channels—including radio, posters, cinema, newspapers, books, art and theater—are vehicles for false ideology's deadly infections.

Although all spirits work on our minds, Behemoth is a mammoth of mind control. Think about it for a minute. How do false religions or political movements spread? How do they gain ground? Through our own individual belief systems. Media can propagate the message, but unless we believe it as individuals, it cannot take root in a city, region, or nation to create a bronze heaven where God's ideologies are replaced with demonic ideologies.

Breaking Open Bronze Heavens

Deuteronomy 28:15 explains, *"It shall come about, if you do not obey the Lord your God, to observe to do all His commandments and His statutes with which I charge you today, that all these curses will come upon you and overtake you."* We see a number of curses described in detail in the verses that follow, but for our purposes of dismantling Behemoths we need to look at Deuteronomy 28:23: *"The heaven which is over your head shall be bronze, and the earth which is under you, iron."* The New Living Translation says, *"unyielding as bronze."*

As we discussed briefly in the last chapter, Job 20:18 calls Behemoth's bones *"tubes of bronze"* and describes Behemoth's limbs as *"bars of iron."* Is it merely a coincidence that the curse of the law mirrors these terms? No, I don't believe so. I believe disobedience opens the door to Behemoth, among other spirits.

The King James Version uses the word *"brass"* instead of bronze. This is not literal but symbolic. Consider what this Scripture is saying in relation to a Behemoth principality over a region. Behemoth earns a place in the heavenlies over a region that is buying into antichrist ideologies. Bible commentaries consider a bronze heaven to be marked by drought. From a spiritual warfare sense, this doesn't mean a lack of food or water. It points to spiritual drought.

Where Behemoth exercises its muscle, you'll find a Word famine and a spiritual drought that keeps people blinded to the power of God. Discerning believers may recognize a stronghold but often feel as if their prayers are hitting a bronze barrier—that petitions and decrees go up but answers don't come down. Intercessors grow especially weary because the breaker anointing on their prayers isn't producing the expected breakthrough. Over time, even the most fervent intercessors tend to back off from beating their heads against bronze walls.

Breaking open brass heavens requires assistance from the angel armies. We find this principle in the Book of Daniel. Daniel was in Babylon, home to bronze heavens. We find in Scripture Daniel confessing *"extreme weariness"* before the angel Gabriel showed up with a message (see Daniel 9:22). In Daniel 9:22-23 we also read: *"He gave me instruction and talked with me and said, 'O Daniel, I have now come forth to give you insight with understanding. At the beginning of your supplications the command was issued...."*

If Daniel could have seen more deeply into the spirit realm, he would have seen beyond the bronze heaven that was wearing him down. He would have seen the war in the heavens. Daniel's prayers launched as the Lord dispatched a messenger angel followed by a warring angel. An angel bringing the prayer answer was revealed to the prophet in Daniel 10:12-13:

> *...Do not be afraid, Daniel, for from the first day that you set your heart on understanding this and on humbling yourself before your God, your words were heard, and I have come in response to your words. But the prince of the kingdom of Persia was withstanding me for twenty-one days; then behold, Michael, one of the chief princes, came to help me, for I had been left there with the kings of Persia.*

Daniel's prayers penetrated the bronze heaven, rallied angels, and led to a visitation that is recorded in the Bible for all to see. While we mainly focus on the end-times revelation in this passage, we would do well to encourage ourselves in intercession by Daniel's success in breaking open a bronze heaven. Daniel, though weary, did not give up. He kept praying and fasting and repenting until his prayers released enough power to penetrate the brass above him. What we saw here was God Himself operating in the truth of Isaiah 45:2: *"I will shatter the doors of bronze and cut through their iron bars."*

God hears your prayers in a bronze heaven—even a heaven where Behemoth has built a brassy stronghold. Persistence is the key to breaking open brass heavens. Consider Christ's parable of the widow in Luke 18:1-8:

> *Now He was telling them a parable to show that at all times they ought to pray and not to lose heart, saying, "In a certain city there was a judge who did not fear God and did not respect man. There was a widow in that city, and she kept coming to him, saying, 'Give me legal protection from my opponent.' For a while he was unwilling; but afterward he said to himself, 'Even though I do not fear God nor respect man, yet because*

this widow bothers me, I will give her legal protection, otherwise by continually coming she will wear me out.'" And the Lord said, "Hear what the unrighteous judge said; now, will not God bring about justice for His elect who cry to Him day and night, and will He delay long over them? I tell you that He will bring about justice for them quickly. However, when the Son of Man comes, will He find faith on the earth?"

And again, consider Jesus' words in Luke 11:5-10:

Suppose one of you has a friend, and goes to him at midnight and says to him, "Friend, lend me three loaves; for a friend of mine has come to me from a journey, and I have nothing to set before him"; and from inside he answers and says, "Do not bother me; the door has already been shut and my children and I are in bed; I cannot get up and give you anything." I tell you, even though he will not get up and give him anything because he is his friend, yet because of his persistence he will get up and give him as much as he needs. So I say to you, ask, and it will be given to you; seek, and you will find; knock, and it will be opened to you. For everyone who asks, receives; and he who seeks, finds; and to him who knocks, it will be opened.

If you keep knocking in prayer, the bronze heavens will be opened. Do not grow weary in well doing because you will see a harvest of breakthrough if you don't give up (see Galatians 6:9). Pray without ceasing (see 1 Thessalonians 5:17). Know that, even in the face of Behemoths, 1 John 5:15 is true: *"And if we know that He hears us in whatever we ask, we know that we have the requests which we have asked from Him."*

Most of all, remember bronze heavens are connected to a curse—and we're not called to live under a curse. Galatians 3:13-15 assures us, *"Christ redeemed us from the curse of the Law, having become a curse for us—for it is written, 'Cursed is everyone who hangs on a tree'—in order that in Christ Jesus the blessing of Abraham might come to the Gentiles, so that we would receive the promise of the Spirit through faith."* Be like Daniel. Keep praying.

You Can Pull Down a Behemoth

Like Babylon will fall one day, Behemoths can fall. Believers can tear them down. It starts, again, in the hearts and minds of the people oppressed by these ideologies. It starts with a personal awakening that drives a great awakening.

While the Behemoth of communism led to the formation of the Soviet Union in 1921—as *History.com* describes "the world's first Marxist-Communist state would become one of the biggest and most powerful nations in the world, occupying nearly one-sixth of the Earth's land surface before its fall in 1991—the period of Red Terror ended, the Cold War ended and political revolution ensued."[1] The Berlin Wall—a wall that separated East and West Germany—was torn down. And millions were set free from Behemoth's stronghold in deed if not in mind.

Eckhardt writes:

> Communism was an antichrist system that controlled hundreds of millions. But this system has been shaken and continues to fall. The head of this system (U.S.S.R.) has crumbled economically and politically, and now the gospel is being preached in Russia, and churches are springing up everywhere. For years the church prayed and fasted for the dismantling of this behemoth, and now we see the results of our prayers.

Thankfully, the Lord is raising up an army of believers who understand spiritual warfare and will challenge and pull down the behemoths of our day. Yet the church must realize that when we are dealing with Behemoth, we are fighting a demonic system that is large and strong, whether it be religious, economic, cultural or political. Many believers who engage in spiritual warfare have accurately identified strongholds in a city, region or even nation; and in fact, stronghold has become a common term among Christians. But it's time the church woke up and recognized that there are some strongholds in various parts of the world that are behemoths—and this size alone should cause us to seek deeper understanding and revelation from the Lord on how to deal with them in spiritual warfare.[2]

While you can pull down a Behemoth, it's not a task to try alone. It's not an overnight prayer meeting. It's persistent corporate prayer over time—but it's also a matter of letting your light shine and spreading the Gospel of Jesus Christ. Ultimately, this battle is the Lord's.

Cindy Trimm writes in her book, *Rules of Engagement: The Art of Strategic Prayer and Spiritual Warfare:*

The Book of Job graphically depicts the spiritual powers and strength of these principalities as unconquerable by human ingenuity. I caution readers to ensure that they are fighting within their measure of rule and fighting under divine covering. Do not go head-to-head with this principality. Allow spiritual generals to initiate and orchestrate prayer and spiritual warfare activities concerning these spirits. Remember to pray under divine covering!... We must implore Jehovah-Gibbor to divinely cause their sinews to be rippled and their bones to be crushed.[3]

A Prayer to Battle Behemoths

Father, I thank You that when I confess my sins You are faithful and just to forgive me of all my sins and cleanse me from all unrighteousness. Forgive me, Lord, for embracing ideologies that defy Your Kingdom way and rule. Forgive me, Father, for rebelling in any measure against Your authority, in Jesus' name. I know Your thoughts are higher than my thoughts and Your ways are higher than My ways. Show me Your ways and teach me Your paths.

Father, deliver me from systematical Behemoth mindsets that have influenced my thoughts, words, and deeds. Loose me from any and all ties to Behemoth spirits that cross land and sea. Help me to renew my mind with Your Word in any area Behemoth may be successfully speaking to my heart. Teach me to discern this spirit's voice so I can cast it down, in Jesus' name.

Father, angels hearken to the voice of Your word. So I ask You to release Your ministering spirits—Your warfare angels—to do battle in the heavenlies with Behemoths over cities and nations. God, the battle belongs to You. Tear down the walls Behemoth has built. Let Your Gospel light penetrate the minds of people groups around the world who are in bondage to Behemoth's diabolical agendas.

Raise up a people who will fight with wisdom and preach with mercy. Let revival come in nations where Behemoth has held people in lifeless forms of religion. I decree and declare Behemoths must fall to Your truth, in Jesus' name.

Endnotes

1. *History*, "Soviet Union"; http://www.history.com/topics/history-of-the-soviet-union; accessed April 21, 2018.

2. John Eckhardt, "Battling the Behemoths of Our Time," *CharismaMagazine*, December 1, 2014; https://www.charismamag.com/spirit/spiritu-

al-warfare/21554-battling-the-behemoths-of-our-time; accessed April 21, 2018.

3. Cindy Trimm, *Rules of Engagement: The Art of Strategic Prayer and Spiritual Warfare* (Lake Mary, FL: Charisma House, 2008), 169.

Chapter 16

RELEASING
THE KINGDOM

MARINE demons are no more dangerous than any other demon power in spiritual warfare in theory and theology. But they are proving to be especially dangerous in spiritual warfare realities and practicalities because we are less familiar with the devil's devices in the waters. For most Christians, water spirits are unseen and unknown—out of sight and out of mind.

Armed with an awareness of marine demons, you should not be afraid. Rather, you should be confident because you have understanding and authority. God will give you the discernment to recognize the operations of these wily water spirits and resist them in His name. Indeed, you can lean on James 4:7—submit yourself to God, resist the devil and he will flee.

Marine demons may seem foreign because we don't run into them every day. But water spirits are no match for the Holy Spirit and God's holy angels.

While we cannot completely do away with water spirits—or any other spirits—until Jesus comes back for the ultimate battle and the final world conflict against satan and his demons, we can push them back over our lives and over our cities. We can change the spiritual climates over our lives, our

---

families, and our towns. We can invite the Holy Spirit to rule and reign and displace water spirits and hybrid spirits that roam the earth and sea.

Shifting the Climate Over Your Life

Of course, you can't shift the spiritual climate over your city until you shift the spiritual climate over your life. We can't take corporate authority over demons in our cities until we have strong, stable believers who can take authority over the demons attacking their minds.

When water spirits—or any spirits—are attacking your life, it creates a climate of fear, discouragement, doubt, and other ungodly thoughts and emotions. If you want to shift from overwhelming warfare to overwhelming victory, you need to create a climate that sets the stage for God to move in your life.

Scientists will tell you that the earth's seasons have shifted in recent years— and they point to climate change as the foundation for the shift. What is a climate? According to *Merriam-Webster*, a climate is "the average course or condition of the weather at a place usually over a period of years as exhibited by temperature, wind velocity and precipitation."

If we translate this to spiritual realities, we learn that the spiritual climate over your life may take years to establish. For example, the enemy can't establish a climate of fear over your life with one "Boo." Much the same, the Holy Spirit can't establish a climate of intimacy over your life with one hour of fellowship every once in a while. By definition, developing a climate of any kind takes time.

Natural climates manifest through temperature. It takes time for Christians to become lukewarm. It tends to happen little by little. It takes time for Christians to catch the fire of God and turn red hot. It may seem like these things happen overnight or in an instant, but the reality is both God and the enemy are at work in our lives. If we give the Holy Spirit permission, He will spark a fire in us that grows to a raging inferno of passion for Jesus. If we give the devil access, he will quench our fire and passion for God.

Both of these spiritual scenarios happen little by little until we reach a tipping point where we feel or discern the shift in our minds and hearts. In other words, we may not feel ourselves growing hungrier for God or losing our passion for Jesus until one day we're hot or cold. The good news is, even if you are cold God can set you on fire again. You can change the spiritual climate over your life.

Natural climates are marked by wind velocity. Wind is one symbol for the Holy Spirit. Velocity is the speed at which something moves. When the devil's winds slam against your house, it brings drama, trauma, and possible destruction—unless your house is built on Christ (see Matthew 7:27). When the Holy Spirit's wind blows, we see life emerge in situations that seem hopeless, refreshing come to the weary, the love of God manifest in our midst, and even signs, wonders, healing, and miracles.

Natural climates are marked by precipitation. Precipitation is rain, sleet, snow, mist, or hail. The enemy brings storms in our life, but God brings restoration in the face of barrenness and loss. The Bible speaks of the former rain and the latter rain (see Joel 2:23) in terms of refreshing where there have been dry or barren seasons. The outpouring on the day of Pentecost is part of the latter rain. When the Holy Spirit pours out rain, He's pouring out hope.

What Is the Spiritual Climate Over Your Life?

If we again translate all this to a spiritual reality—as natural surroundings often correspond to spiritual conditions—it's clear that changing our spiritual climate sets the stage for a shift in spiritual seasons. We can't shift our seasons—God does that. But we can create a climate that invites Him to do the work in our hearts that prepares us for the next season—we can move from a season of oppressive warfare to a season of oppressive victory.

What is the spiritual climate over your life? If you are angry, ungrateful, complaining, angry, greedy, controlling, critical, impatient, indifferent, discouraged, jealous, frightened, frustrated, unforgiving, resentful, bitter, selfish, or something of the like, you're creating a spiritual climate over your life that repels the Holy Spirit. He loves you, yes, but your flesh is warring against His Spirit.

If, by contrast, you are thankful, peaceful, prayerful, joyful, generous, forgiving, loving, content, self-less, hopeful, faithful, inspired, and worshipful, you are creating an atmosphere that attracts the presence of God. And the presence of the Holy Spirit is the ultimate key to spiritual change and growth. Put another way, we need to cultivate the fruit of the Spirit in our lives and reject the works of the flesh. In doing so, we position our hearts for God to shift us into fruitful seasons of harvest.

In her book *Shifting Atmospheres: A Strategy for Victorious Spiritual Warfare*—a book I wholeheartedly endorse—Dawna DeSilva writes:

> Some people believe that ungodly atmospheres are the same thing as demonic spirits. While I do believe demonic atmospheres are presided over by the demonic realm, I do not believe the atmospheres themselves are actual demons. Atmospheres, for me, are the prevailing spiritual realities created by man's partnership with the entities residing in the spiritual realm. As the messages these spiritual beings emit are agreed upon and partnered with, the resulting atmosphere expands. Therefore, I see atmospheres, both godly and ungodly, as cyclical partnerings between broadcasts from the spirit realm and man's participation with them....[1]

Shifting the Spiritual Climate Over Your City

Some of the principles of shifting the spiritual climate over your life apply directly to shifting the spiritual climate over your city—but on a corporate level.

I don't know where you live. I live in South Florida where the *spiritual climate* often seems as hard as bronze. (Bronze heavens are part of the curse of the law, according to Deuteronomy 28:23, as we discussed in an earlier chapter). South Florida is sometimes called the "evangelist's graveyard." The **spiritual climate** is intense.

Sometimes, it seems like our **prayers** hit a bronze ceiling and fall back down to the earth again. Of course, we know that's not true because God hears the **prayers** of the righteous (see Proverbs 15:8). But prayer often feels like a heated battle when you are in a tight **spiritual climate** with strongholds like **witchcraft** and **Jezebel**. Sometimes you don't even feel like praying. In her book, DeSilva writes:

> Many of us have experienced spiritually 'thin' places or open heavens. These are areas where the accumulation of worship and prayer has released the tangible presence of God. In these places, healings, salvations, signs, and wonders are more easily attained than in more spiritually 'thick' areas. These thick places are environments where negative spiritual climates have been allowed to develop. In areas governed by a religious spirit, for instance, the prophetic tends to not flow as freely.
>
> I see the development of negative atmospheres as a result of people partnering with sin, lies, or the demonic. As humans partner with these things, more and more evil spirits are attracted. This results in the development of a negative spiritual climate from which demonic forces can operate. ...The

more people agree with these evil spirits and their messages through partnerships with sin, the more powerful the atmospheres become. This is how strongholds develop.

Strongholds, areas of particular resistance, grow as people partner with lies, sin, and demonic broadcasts. Whether these broadcasts are transmissions of fear, hate, perversion, or self-loathing, they weaken a person's spiritual and emotional health and cause havoc.

When evil spirits gain a place of power over a region, they broadcast lies over the entire area—much like a radio station. We have the capacity to either "tune in" to these channels or to switch them off. Part of our responsibility in tuning out the enemy's voice is for us to switch the channel we are listening to that is emitting a sinful broadcast, but doing so does not actually shut off its transmissions into the airwaves. We need to release God's opposing messages into the airwaves to actually stop these transmissions.[2]

Amen.

Jesus Shifted Climates Everywhere He Went

We see spiritual climate shifts in the Bible that build our faith. Jesus shifted the climate and released the kingdom over the sea. We read the account in Mark 4:35-41:

> *On that day, when evening came, He said to them, "Let us go over to the other side." Leaving the crowd, they took Him along with them in the boat, just as He was; and other boats were with Him. And there arose a fierce gale of wind, and the waves were breaking over the boat so much that the boat was already*

filling up. Jesus Himself was in the stern, asleep on the cushion; and they woke Him and said to Him, "Teacher, do You not care that we are perishing?" And He got up and rebuked the wind and said to the sea, "Hush, be still." And the wind died down and it became perfectly calm. And He said to them, "Why are you afraid? Do you still have no faith?" They became very much afraid and said to one another, "Who then is this, that even the wind and the sea obey Him?"

Jesus has delegated His authority to you to release the Kingdom everywhere you go. The Kingdom of God is within you (see Luke 17:21). He's given us a command to "occupy" until He comes back (see Luke 19:13). The Greek word for "occupy" is *pragmateunmai,* which means "to be occupied in anything, to carry on a business," according to *The KJV New Testament Greek Lexicon.* Jesus was always about His Father's business (Luke 2:49). Jesus only did what He saw the Father do (see John 5:19).

You might say, "Well, that was Jesus." But Christ is in you. When the enemy comes in with a storm, we have the authority to shift the spiritual climate—and we have the responsibility to because we are Christ's ambassadors on the earth. Christ wasn't the only man to walk the earth and shift spiritual climates. Elijah shifted the natural climate and spiritual climate over the city. We read about this in 1 Kings.

King Ahab and his wife Jezebel took the tradition of kings calling on prophets to unlock the mysteries of god a step further—and a few steps too far. Jezebel had false prophets on her payroll. The wicked queen regularly fed 450 prophets of Baal and 400 prophets of Asherah. Bible scholars estimate that feeding those false prophets cost her about $12,750 a week or $663,000 a year. That's a hefty price tag for a good prophetic word.

While Jezebel's prophets had full bellies in a time of famine, the queen cut off the prophets of the Lord for fear of the truth (see 1 Kings 18:4). Obadiah hid 100 of God's prophets in caves and fed them bread and water. While

Jezebel's prophets looked well-fed and God's true prophets looked like sheep being led to the slaughter, the story changes in a hurry when Elijah confronts the 850 merchandisers at Mount Carmel in what goes down in biblical history as the ultimate showdown between the true and the false. Elijah threw down the prophetic gauntlet and challenged the false camp to bring fire down from heaven by calling upon their god. The merchandising diviners cried to Baal from dawn to dusk with no answer.

When the false camp had finally exhausted itself, Elijah built an altar holding a sacrifice to Jehovah, drenched it with four barrels of water, said a simple prayer, and watched as the fire of God fell from heaven and consumed the sacrifice, the wood, the stones, the dust, and even the water in the trench. Then Elijah slew his false counterparts one by one. So the ultimate fate of the false prophets came at the hand of the true prophet, who was later taken to heaven in a chariot of fire. Then we saw a climate shift that brought relief from the famine. We read this miraculous account in 1 Kings 18:41-45:

> *Now Elijah said to Ahab, "Go up, eat and drink; for there is the sound of the roar of a heavy shower." So Ahab went up to eat and drink. But Elijah went up to the top of Carmel; and he crouched down on the earth and put his face between his knees. He said to his servant, "Go up now, look toward the sea." So he went up and looked and said, "There is nothing." And he said, "Go back" seven times. It came about at the seventh time, that he said, "Behold, a cloud as small as a man's hand is coming up from the sea." And he said, "Go up, say to Ahab, 'Prepare your chariot and go down, so that the heavy shower does not stop you.'" In a little while the sky grew black with clouds and wind, and there was a heavy shower....*

Notice the climate didn't shift immediately upon the demonic climate being displaced. But once the demonic agenda was displaced—once the Israelites agreed to serve the Lord and reject the Baals—it paved a clear path for

Elijah to pray in relief from the drought. Once demons are cast out, we still have to invite the Holy Spirit in. We can't just sweep the house clean without asking the Holy Spirit to fill the house or demons will come back again.

Jesus said:

> *Now when the unclean spirit goes out of a man, it passes through waterless places seeking rest, and does not find it. Then it says, "I will return to my house from which I came"; and when it comes, it finds it unoccupied, swept, and put in order. Then it goes and takes along with it seven other spirits more wicked than itself, and they go in and live there; and the last state of that man becomes worse than the first...* (Matthew 12:43-46).

Jesus was speaking to an individual's deliverance, but the same principle applies to cities.

You might say, "Well, that was Elijah. He was a miracle-working prophet. Of course, he could shift the spiritual climate." Let me give you another perspective from James, the apostle of practical faith:

> *...The effective prayer of a righteous man can accomplish much. Elijah was a man with a nature like ours, and he prayed earnestly that it would not rain, and it did not rain on the earth for three years and six months. Then he prayed again, and the sky poured rain and the earth produced its fruit* (James 5:16-18).

Elijah wasn't perfect, but God used him. The Spirit that raised Christ from the dead dwells in you (see Romans 8:11). You can do all things through Christ who strengthens you (see Philippians 4:13).

Practical Keys for Shifting Atmospheres and Releasing the Kingdom

Entire books have been written on shifting atmospheres and releasing the Kingdom. In a nutshell, you shift an atmosphere through a combination of several tactics—always led by the Holy Spirit. Remember, it's the Holy Spirit who gives us revelation on which key to use at any given time.

We know that prayer changes things. In order to shift an atmosphere, we should first go straight to God. God is the ultimate shifter and can shift things we don't even discern. Start by asking God to break in with light and love and shift an atmosphere of darkness and hate. Ask God to break in with joy and freedom where depression and oppression are lingering. Ask God to break in with peace where strife exists. You get the picture.

We can also prophesy God's will to the heavens. We can decree, declare, and proclaim the Word of God. We can praise and worship our way into a new atmosphere. On the spiritual warfare front, we can bind and loose enemy powers. We can plead the blood of Jesus. We can do prophetic acts, as led by the Spirit. We can open and close doors with the Isaiah 22:22 Scripture, exercising our governing authority. Isaiah 22:22 says, *"Then I will set the key of the house of David on his shoulder, when he opens no one will shut, when he shuts no one will open."* I write about all of these prophetic warfare strategies in my book, *Waging Prophetic Warfare*.

We can release the Kingdom by walking in love (see Ephesians 5:2). Moreover, we can release the Kingdom by operating in the fruit of the Spirit, which in addition to love includes joy, peace, patience, kindness, goodness, faithfulness, gentleness, self-control (see Galatians 5:22-23). We can release the Kingdom by stepping out in faith with the gifts of the Spirit—which are the word of wisdom, the word of knowledge, the gift of faith, the gifts of healing, the working of miracles, the gift of prophecy, the discerning of spirits, and tongues and interpretation of tongues (see 1 Corinthians 12:8-10)—to demonstrate God's power.

Remember, the Kingdom of God dwells in you (see Luke 17:21). And in 1 Corinthians 4:20, Paul asserts, *"For the kingdom of God does not consist in words but in power."*

Endnotes

1. Dawna DeSilva, *Shifting Atmospheres: A Strategy for Victorious Spiritual Warfare* (Shippensburg, PA: Destiny Image Publishers, 2017).

2. Ibid.

Conclusion

Armed with the information and revelation in this book, you are prepared to battle against unseen marine demons that will flee just like any other demon that attacks you. Refer back to this book often in the midst of warfare for a refresher course on these marine spirits.

Although the Holy Spirit should always be your guide, I believe He has and will use the pages of this book to show you what you need to see in the thick of the battle—to remind you of those "aha moments" you had while you read the words on these pages.

But, please, stay balanced. Remember Peter's admonition in 1 Peter 5:8 AMPC. What do I mean? Well, now that you're well-versed in the world of water spirits, you will undoubtedly begin to discern spiritually and naturally the operations of marine demons. Before you close the cover of this book, I want you to hear this loud and clear—*it's important that you **discern** and not **presume** in the spirit world. Presumption and assumption about spirits can open the door to warfare from demons that didn't have you on their radar screen.*

Let me also remind you of a warfare faux pas straight from my own life. When I first learned about the spirit of Jezebel, I thought everything was a Jezebel spirit. When my computer crashed, I pointed an angry finger at

Jezebel. When I had a flat tire, I hollered out loud, binding Jezebel. When anything and everything went wrong, I was convinced Jezebel was the culprit.

This is what is called a spiritual warfare ditch—and you want to avoid it at all costs because you are at a spiritual warfare disadvantage in a ditch. Anytime you rely on book smarts alone and leave the Holy Spirit's voice out of your battle plans, you're risking retaliation you won't soon forget—and didn't have to face.

Yes, it's absolutely true God always leads us into triumph in Christ (see 2 Corinthians 2:14)—but we have to let Him lead us. When we lead ourselves or follow someone else's wisdom rather than pressing in for our own revelation about what is attacking we can meet with resistance we're not expecting. So, stay alert, watch and pray, and keep your ear to the Holy Spirit's heart.

Also remember that the same general spiritual warfare rules apply to battling any demon. The crux of spiritual warfare is submitting yourself to God and resisting the devil (see James 4:7).

That starts in our mind, most of the time. It's hard to resist something you don't discern, so spiritual warfare books that expose the operations of various spirits are helpful in training yourself in discernment. It's up to you to fight the good fight of faith consistently knowing that you will win if you follow the Spirit. Even if you lose a battle, you will ultimately win the war. Keep fighting!

I pray that your discernment and revelation have increased through the pages of this book and that the Lord will continue to pour out a spirit of wisdom and revelation and increase your spiritual discernment, in Jesus' name. I loose ministering angels around and about you—warring angels who hearken to God's Word coming out of your mouth. I pray protection over you as you set out to put some new enemies under your feet—enemies you may not even have known you had until you read this book. I break every curse off your life and call you blessed, in Jesus' name. Amen.

About the Author

Jennifer LeClaire is the senior leader of Awakening House of Prayer in Fort Lauderdale, Florida, founder of the Ignite Network and founder of the Awakening Blaze prayer movement. She formerly served as the first female editor of *Charisma* magazine and is a prolific author of more than 25 books.

You can find Jennifer online or send her an email at info@jenniferleclaire.org.

Notes